Modigliani · Drawings and Sketches

# MODIGLIANI

## DRAWINGS AND SKETCHES

FRANCO RUSSOLI
*Director, The Brera Gallery, Milan*

HARRY N. ABRAMS, INC. · PUBLISHERS · NEW YORK

Text translated by John Shepley

Standard Book Number: 8109-0324-5
Library of Congress Catalogue Card Number: 69-14193
Copyright 1969 in Germany by Verlag Gerd Hatje, Stuttgart
Harry N. Abrams, Incorporated, New York
Printed and bound in Germany
Picture reproduction rights reserved by ADAGP, Paris, and Cosmopress, Geneva

Drawing is the fundamental element in Modigliani's search for expression and in all of his stylistic achievements. His poetic vision, whether carried out in the form of painting or sculpture, first takes shape and finds its essential definition in graphic terms. The two dialectical poles of his personality—the artist's sensual and psychological attraction to the *individual* in all his physical and emotional reality, and his aspiration as a symbolist and formalist to express this existential reality in the abbreviated image, the formula of style—are both obvious in his countless drawings.

There are quick sketches from life and character impressions, as well as many examples where the artist was seeking a pure structure of forms or the abstract harmony of contours and arabesques. In many more drawings, however, these preliminary and functional aspects complement each other and merge in a formal image whose crystalline coherence resolves the visual and emotional complexities presented by the model. These drawings are sufficient to demonstrate, not only the value, but the fundamental nature of Modigliani's art. His paintings and sculpture reveal no additional essential aspects of his vision and style, but rather are parallel expressions, in different media, of the same principles and artistic discoveries. Their range of expression is wider and more varied, but the formulation of the image in its unity of representation and style remains unaltered.

Far be it from me to detract from the importance of Modigliani's paintings or sculptures; I only wish to stress that their chromatic, material, and plastic qualities are the elaboration, and at times the enrichment, of a graphic solution already arrived at. The intense, subtle color and the volumetric structure of Modigliani's figures, so clearly articulated in space, are implicit in his variations of light and shading, and in his rhythm of line, now terse and biting, now vanishing in the luminous void of the paper, now spreading out into thick streaks and blots. As Lamberto Vitali has justly observed: "The future fate of Modigliani, whatever it may be, can well be entrusted to a single one of his drawings."

Even so, there is a persistent tendency to sum up Modigliani's style as a combination of psychologizing and sensual grace, a synthesis of melodious Neo-Gothic contours and elegantly mannered forms. And despite many perceptive historical interpretations of his work, which recently have emphasized the cultural complexity, the stages of development in his artistic career, many still think of Modigliani as the isolated and spontaneous singer appearing suddenly

V

in Montparnasse to revive the melodies of the Tuscan Renaissance, and creating out of his romantic and Jewish despair and the pathos of a *poète maudit* a pure image, that of a rootless flower blooming in a hothouse of timeless lyricism.

It seems to me that a critical examination of his drawings, in an attempt to establish their chronological order and link them to his painting and sculpture, can contribute to an understanding of the real complexity behind his artistic mission. These splendid works are incontrovertible evidence of Modigliani's participation in the artistic vicissitudes of his time, and of his active exploration of new modes of expression. Although he did not attach himself to specific movements or to the experimental avant-garde, being perhaps convinced of the historical continuity of artistic development as it reflects the relationship between man and reality, he was nevertheless receptive to the most revolutionary innovations in style.

He was not so much concerned with poetic generalizations and broad interpretations of the universe as with formal matters, the pure facts of "seeing" and "expression." The problem of style was his prime concern; his work carries no social or philosophical message. His world was highly individual and lyrical, involving a profound attachment to man and a yearning for eternal spirituality embodied in harmonious and vibrant form. "*Je forgerai une coupe et cette coupe sera le réceptacle de ma Passion.*" His refusal to sign the Futurist Manifesto is well known, as are his original "approximations" of Cézanne, Picasso, Matisse, Klimt, Derain, and Brancusi, to whose work he turned for examples, as also to the culture of antiquity and of the African and Oceanic peoples.

Modigliani did not create the elements of a new mode of expression, as did the Fauves and Cubists, for example, but neither did he adhere passively to traditional or modern formulas. From any living form, or any stylistic suggestion, he knew how to draw the inspiration necessary to his own highly personal idiom, which fuses existential reality with the ideal classicism of pure formal structure (and is imitable only as a manneristic exercise). Modigliani achieved his style only by this continuous critical participation in the growth of the contemporary artistic idiom, and not by a miraculous resurrection of "Tuscan" measure and elegance. He was no naïve heir to a mythical tradition, but a schooled artist deeply committed to the culture of his time. The best proof of this is offered by his drawings.

There are very few of Modigliani's drawings that can be dated before 1907. Aside from the academic studies in the Leghorn Museum, the pastel portrait of his friend Fabio Mauroner executed in Venice in 1905, the Parisian drawing of 1907 of Mario Buggelli in a café (Plate 3), and the drawings in the Alexandre and Biddle collections we cannot cite

any other with certainty except a *Head of a Woman* in a private collection in Paris, the style of which would place it about 1906-7.

Since almost all the artist's undoubtedly varied and abundant graphic production of those years of study and uncertain development has been dispersed, it would be hazardous to venture any critical hypothesis on Modigliani's early drawings. From the examples mentioned and the characteristics of the equally scarce paintings from this period, we can conclude only that the young artist, in his transition from a timid naturalism to a delicate and psychologically-based symbolism, sought to merge an evocative and radiant evanescence with an intense, characteristic line. Subsequently, in the early Paris days, under the influence of the caustic graphic technique of Toulouse-Lautrec and such illustrators as Steinlen, Villon, Forain, and others of *Le Rire* and *L'Assiette au Beurre,* this decisive and fluid line becomes freer and outlines the model in strong Secessionist arabesques. The search for chromatic vibration through a counterpoint of chiaroscuro and linear density is also recognizable in the drawings of 1907.

The following year was a period of extraordinary clarification, of revolutionary discoveries that put Modigliani on the path to knowledge of his own world of expression. The paintings of that time show a sudden burst of maturity, a furious and anxious thrust toward clarity, over many experiments and unexpected triumphs. His twin yearning for dramatic intimacy, a touching humanism compounded of compassion and moral detachment, and for a restless, aristocratic, and decadent symbolism carried him from Carrière and Whistler to Sickert, Beardsley, Klimt, and Munch, and to the Picasso of the Blue and Rose Periods. His vision, increasingly divided between character portraits and raw compositional rhythm, took shape in a synthesis of harsh lines and burning colors, a *cloisonnisme* which with Expressionist fervor translated the incised lines of Art Nouveau and the patches of pure color of the Fauves.

This fretful knot of influences, aspirations, and experiments was loosed by the revelation Modigliani experienced at the Cézanne exhibition. Naturally it was neither an easy nor immediate achievement, and the first effect of the lesson is seen only in a greater severity and serenity of composition, as in the external employment of a dominant blue-green tone, elaborated in its qualities of intrinsic luminosity. But the abandonment of decadent rhetorical rhythms in the structure of his figures and a more coherent fusion of the areas of color in volumes clearly defined in the drawing constituted the first, revolutionary step toward the elimination of literary and decorative excesses. As Lamberto Vitali has observed, the influence of Cézanne was not exerted directly on Modigliani's style, but by revealing the importance of formal classical moderation it helped the Italian artist to find the synthetic and functional power of line. From then on Modigliani's every symbolist tendency, every influence inherited from the Secessionists, such as his inveterate propensity toward exaggerated facial definition and sentimentality, is expressed in a simple and limpid idiom of severe graphic purity.

If Modigliani's study of Cézanne showed him the way to represent individual character in its essential forms and rhythms, without descriptive accents or rhetorical emphasis, his subsequent meeting with Brancusi determined the need to carry this process of simplification and synthesis still further. But it was to be in the direction of an abstract perfection that would be the formal symbol, "the edifice and I might almost say the metaphysical architecture" (as Modigliani had expressed it years before in a letter to his friend Oscar Ghiglia) of Truth revealed through Beauty. Clearly the aestheticizing and symbolist side of his temperament gained the upper hand, his aspiration toward the Absolute as incarnated in the most rarefied harmony of plastic elements.

It was in this sense, too, that he saw Negro, Oriental, and primitive works—as emblems of a marvelous fusion of instinct and stylistic elaboration. Inspired formal invention and the most refined triumph of stylized structure came together and were displayed in the magical and ceremonial objects of the Belgian Congo, in Indian, Egyptian, and Archaic Greek sculpture, and in Gothic and Renaissance works of Tuscany. And the medium of sculpture, by its very roughness, seemed to him the most appropriate means to express that absolute and mythical idea of pure form that contains and exalts all human passions.

In 1909 Modigliani began working on those studies of African sculpture that constitute the first substantial known body of his graphic output. Meanwhile, in his paintings, he continued to develop motifs derived from Cézanne (some of these works were included among those exhibited in 1910 at the Salon des Indépendants), but the decision to devote himself to sculpture became still stronger. Even though in such paintings of 1909 and 1910 as *The Cellist* and the *Female Heads* in the Alexandre Collection, along with the general influence of Cézanne, we can detect particular graphic and plastic solutions obviously derived from the study of Negro sculpture, the final transition to these new stylistic interests did not take place until 1911. For that year, in fact, with the exception of a portrait of Paul Alexandre, we have only drawings and washes with nude studies and heads taken from African sculpture (Plates 6-12), or exercises in the more decorative aspects of those orientalizing forms favored by the Secessionist and Art Nouveau schools.

In 1912 Modigliani exhibited at the Salon d'Automne a group of seven sculptures under the all-inclusive and revealing title *Têtes, ensemble décoratif*. A comparison of these and others of the same period with their preliminary drawings confirms Vitali's judgment that "Modigliani the new draftsman was born from Modigliani the sculptor." Indeed, in his pursuit of clear surfaces, precise volumes, and continuous lines curving in space, and his recovery through line

of the values of depth, the interlocking of solids and voids which by their simplified plastic conventions determine the "deformations" of Gabonese and Congolese sculpture, Modigliani reduced line to its utmost simplicity and discovered, as Ceroni says, "the value of pure line, traced always without hesitation, without *pentimenti,* perfect and at once original." The example of Brancusi's drawings, tautly rendering the perfection of volume in what John Russell has called a "ferocious exclusion of the irrelevant," must have been of no small help to him, as was also the lean, free synthesis achieved by the Cubists. The old arabesques of the English and Viennese *fin de siècle,* as well as Cézanne's volumetric syntheses, were brought to new and unexpected results in this exercise in the formal interpretation of primitive art.

This sureness of line and highly sensitive technique of varying its thickness and density to attain certain plastic and chromatic effects, already recognizable in the few drawings we have from the previous years, found a much wider range of application in this series of *Heads* dating from 1909-11. Here we see all the budding elements of Modigliani's graphic style, which will be developed in the wealth of his later production. In the African studies the artist observes and explores primarily the bizarre harmony among spherical, elliptical, and cylindrical forms with the introduction in their midst of vertical elements, that is to say, the subtle interplay of ovals, sudden relief areas, convexities, and rhythmic lines. The conventional and emblematic formulas by which the African sculptors transformed the human figure into an "idol" are interpreted by Modigliani as structural plastic values filtered through his taste for symbolism and the *Jugendstil.* The Archaic Greek canon translates the obsessive figures of black magic into images of abstract and arcane purity. Mindful of this sculptural transformation, Modigliani in his drawings attempts different effects of proportion and relief: now the line disintegrates into almost minuscule dashes to render the vibration of contours and surfaces, now it is supple and firm to show the unfolding of pure volumes in space. Or it becomes sharp, almost like silverpoint, accompanied by soft shadings, to restore a sense of the crystalline clarity of stone and polished wood. Cleanly inscribed on the white of the page or set off by strong vibrant borders, the drawings seem ever-changing and alive. In the sculptures belonging to the Barnes Foundation in Merion, Pennsylvania, in the Museums of Modern Art of New York and Paris, the Philadelphia Museum, the Tate Gallery in London, and in various private American and European collections (illustrated in *Modigliani the Sculptor* by Alfred Werner, New York, 1962), one can see how the preliminary drawings dictated not only the general shape of the figure but also the choice of stylistic solutions.

Between 1911 and 1912 Modigliani continued to find sources in African art for his standing and squatting nudes: female idols and the supports of ceremonial stools (Plates 13, 14, 18). There are two or three paintings and many drawings and watercolors, as well as one sculpture in the Gustave Schindler Collection in New York, to document this period. That fusion, which we noted in the heads, of descriptive analyses of the African image and formal abstract elaboration is also evident in these works. And where the drawing departs most freely from the model, this statement by Agnes Mongan fully applies: "Elliptical, economical, and elusive, his line is yet concise and eloquent" (cf. Bibl. 45). It is a clean line that both cuts and encloses well-defined volumes. But the inspiration furnished by the African "caryatids" took on a life of its own, becoming the starting point for an ambitious and fantastic project, a complex plastic and architectonic composition which would in itself sum up every aesthetic and ideal value: the Temple of Beauty. Its caryatids were thus to combine every emotional, symbolic, and formal element—to the characteristics deduced from African figures, and those derived from the abstract purism of Brancusi and the volumetric distortions of Nadelman, were to be joined Neo-Gothic decorative rhythm, the sensual grace of ancient Indian sculpture, the massive power of Romanesque synthesis, and the Cubists' dynamic simultaneity of vision. The old and the new were to merge in that mythical symbol of Beauty. For years Modigliani was to pursue this dream, seeking in dozens of watercolors, pastels, and drawings that pure and perfect form, the "receptacle" of human passion and tenderness. Even when, probably because of poor health, he abandoned sculpture, he returned in his drawings to the variation and elaboration of the "caryatid" theme (Colorplates following pages VI and X, Plates 19-22). In fact, a number of these drawings correspond stylistically to later periods in his painting, while the one remaining sculpture, now in the Museum of Modern Art in New York, can be dated around 1914.

It is extremely difficult to establish a chronological succession for these drawings. There is a continual and baffling transition from isolated forms, in contrasting and compact masses, to others that wind in soft chiaroscuro on delicate backgrounds of color. The same can be said of the line, now decisive and broken, now flowing in a continuous arabesque like a melodious sequence in the void. Sometimes it is applied with the brush, or flakes off in luminous particles as though to show the image emerging and taking shape from the light and the primordial indistinctness of nature. By referring to the paintings and to trends current in the art world of Paris at the time, we can perhaps propose the following progression: from the drawings in which the influence of African sculpture is the strongest, to those in which the influence of Picasso, "the Romanesque Catalan," and the Cubists is felt, and finally to those where form dissolves in various ways into sensual plastic rhythms and embellishments of a decadent, orientalizing stamp. What is certain is that in the complex and lyrical development of his theme, Modigliani fully demonstrated the wealth of his graphic talent and his extraordinary capacity to endow the simplest and purest elements of drawing with new creative power.

If in his variations on an "abstract" theme, like the emblematic caryatid nude, Modigliani demonstrated such richness of stylistic invention as to give form to the most subtle distinctions of symbolic meaning, one can well imagine the range of graphic expression that was now open to him in portraying real human figures and individual faces. In 1914 Modigliani resumed painting, and he painted portraits. That pure figurative symbol, harmonious and complete in itself, that he had dreamed of crystallizing in the caryatid sculptures and the Temple of Beauty, he now saw within his grasp and so much the richer with life in the individual human image. The facial and psychological traits of a real person were to be the starting point for the creation of forms to be filtered through the screen of stylistic abstraction. The meeting of beauty and truth finally takes place, outside the aestheticizing myth, on the historical plane of the stylistic transfiguration of man's appearance and feeling. From then on the portrait became the emblem of Modigliani's fantasy, both pretext and condition of his art. And once again his drawings offer the best testimony. Even when the artist defines every physical detail, or stresses sentiment, line is always "ideal" line, bearing the development and harmony of surface and volume, an arabesque dictated by its own rhythms. And, as Claude Roy has noted (cf. Bibl. 22). it is the model's personality that gives life and definition to this infinite variety of graphic solutions and prevents them from being merely decorative. The formal manner is based on an intensely realistic interpretation of objective fact, Without succumbing to the technical virtuosity of eclecticism or to representations of the "typical," Modigliani in every instance creates the graphic expression corresponding to the essence of his subject, and still maintains an intimate coherence of vision in his variations of symbol and image. It is not a question of simplification, but of a profound stylistic personality.

Even his references to various contemporary artistic idioms, which, as we mentioned, Modigliani studied with penetrating intelligence, are not systematic, but functional and immediately integrated into a new and entirely original conception. Take, for example, the amazing sketch of 1914 (Michel Grilichess Collection, Paris) for the portrait of Diego Rivera (Plate 45), of which there are two known canvases (cf. Bibl. 6, Plates 31 and 32). At that time Modigliani was trying to graft onto the compact structure of pure form the graphic and chromatic embellishments of Art Nouveau. It is his coherent "mannerist" way of translating stylistically the individual characteristics and objective reality of the figure. After having crystallized his heads, nudes, and caryatids into pure linear and plastic values—first following Brancusian suggestions on African art, and second Picasso's rough synthesis of the Romanesque and the archaic—he seeks in the human figure a new individuality and a new relationship to its surroundings. One sees this in the fusion of chiaroscuro found in some of the caryatids, and even more so in the harmony established between facial expression and formal abstraction in the *Portrait of Frank Haviland,* where the insertion of the contour in the chromatic tessellation is closer to Klimt and the Nabis than to the Fauves. It is in this line of subtle formal interpretation of reality that the Rivera portrait takes its place. From the massive figure of the Mexican painter Modigliani immediately derived the interlocking circular forms of head and body, but instead of carrying them through to an abstract simplification, he makes them only the structural support for an intricate network of graphic embellishments. The line varies in thickness and intensity, curls and dissolves in a series of dots: it is a continuous, virtuoso, and joyous improvisation on the theme of Diego Rivera. Every element is transformed, even the inscription and signature being incorporated into the stylistic embroidery. Here we see how freely and brilliantly he has employed the Viennese graphic repertory, with all the freshness of a frankly human and sensual fidelity to the model, in which, however, any mechanical stiffness of decoration is eliminated.

This quality of vital immediacy and of physical and psychological reality in Modigliani's portraits was nurtured by his constant habit of drawing from life. He practiced an almost obsessive exercise in what Vitali has called "graphic gymnastics," whether elaborating his pure linear and structural inventions or capturing on paper the fleeting, spontaneous aspects of people he knew or met. In his studio, on the street, in the cafés, wherever he found himself Modigliani was forever sketching and taking notes in order to translate what he saw into formal ideas. From this dialectical exercise of representation and elaboration grew an image in which the most acute rendering of the individual reality of the model merged with the freest and most *abstract* stylistic formulation. Once having made the elements of a style his own, Modigliani had recourse to them when the requirements of his model dictated it—they became inextricably a part of his highly personal "manner." Thus we witness a return of arabesques and floral designs in drawings based on a Cubist syntax or on Picasso's manipulation of Ingres: they convey that sudden illumination of detail, that characteristic analytic perception which break the pattern and give life to the image. This can be seen in *Rosa Porprina* (1915, Colorplate following page XVIII) in the Jucker Collection in Milan, or in the *Torso of a Nude Woman* (1917?) in the Brillouin Collection. Partial solutions of the African sort (eyes, noses) likewise reappear to the very last, along with compositional structures reminiscent of Cézanne, the interplay of solids and voids in a Cubist key, and unexpected physiognomical accents in the manner of Toulouse-Lautrec. Modigliani handles with the greatest freedom and coherence all elements of his contemporary figurative culture and those he took from the past—in alternating and composing them he achieves his determination of form based on the elements of nature.

Thus it is extremely difficult to catalogue his drawings or affix to them a critical label. His originality is more pro-

found and elusive, and lies precisely in the capacity to transpose and elevate the individual, atypical aspects of existential reality into a complex harmony of disparate formal symbols.

Between 1915 and 1917 Modigliani produced an uninterrupted succession of drawings in which he achieved the most varied stylistic alchemy. In the portraits of his friends, Picasso (Colorplate following page XIV, Plate 46), Max Jacob (Plate 51), Lipchitz (Plate 52), Laurens, Kisling, Paul Guillaume (Plate 53), Cocteau, Zborowski, Soutine, Moricand (Plate 74), Cendrars, as in those of Beatrice Hastings (Plates 35-37), Lunia Czechowska, and Hanka Zborowska, in the entire gallery of anonymous figures and faces, humble companions of daily life, occasional models and rich patrons, and those images symbolic of sentiments, states of mind, and the human condition (prayer, maternity, love, aristocratic melancholy, open sensuality), the artist always discovers the perfect correspondence between subject and style. Even in the quick sketches from life or the first studies for a painting, his aim is the synthesis of effective characterization and compositional invention. For example, in the *Couple* (Plate 31) in the Alsdorf Collection, the *Portrait of a Man with Hat* (Plate 73) in the Abrams Collection, or *Beatrice Hastings in an Armchair* (Plate 35) in the Vismara Collection, the line is rapid, loose, and open, but while it fixes the image with infallible acuteness and even affectionate irony, the basic elements of the individual characterization already indicate the unfolding of rhythms, planes, and volumes. And in the drawings that are conceived and developed as finished works in themselves, this synthesis is carried to full fruition.

During these years the influence of the artist's sculptural vision is very strong: the plastic and ritual simplifications, passing through a Cubist dissolution, are given over to the interpretation of the subject. They do not condition it, nor are they conditioned by it; they simply embody it pictorially. Modigliani outlines sharply the volumes of heads and bodies, sets them off with passages of soft or vibrant chiaroscuro, makes them stand out either against shadows and dark areas obtained by vertical hatching, or against the white of the page, by the incisive strength of his line. Sometimes the line is interrupted and the descriptive detail eliminated to emphasize the pure formal structure, the intensity of characterization having already been achieved by the focusing of a few elements. Beautiful examples of this stylistic process are the *Portrait of Pablo Picasso* (Plate 46) in the Laporte Collection, the *Seated Woman* (Plate 38) in the Sampliner Collection, and the *Portrait of Beatrice Hastings* (Plate 37) in the Mattioli Collection. But examples would be too numerous, for we should have to mention the many drawings which start out with the same general conception of individualizing character in pure plastic form, but become complicated and enriched by digressions and a repartee of line exploited in all its variations. There are granular outlines, splintered and sawtoothed, set off by others that are limpid and slender, as in *The Passenger—"Transatlantique Boat"* (Plate 43) in the Alsdorf Collection. Or forms are sought in their fleshy plasticity, with curved, broken strokes unexpectedly offset by volumes and planes defined by crystalline lines, without *pentimenti,* and by alternate areas of chiaroscuro, as in the *Seated Young Man* (Plate 39) of the Basel Print Room. In the *Portrait of a Woman* (Plate 63) in the Sainsbury Collection, the Cézanne-like structure and manneristic simplification are freed in a limpid classicizing vein that recalls Ingres as interpreted by Picasso, but with an intonation of melodious and decadent sensibility.

The obsessive stylistic tension and the arduous, complex search for formal solutions seem to abate somewhat in the drawings dating to 1917. There is, in general, an increased reliance on the more "natural" features of the model, and although the definition remains crystalline, it is less elaborated and transformed. The line follows the harmony or asymmetry of the nudes and faces, and is often soft, rhythmic, and simple, without decorative arabesques, as in the *Portrait of Lola* in the Alsdorf Collection. Gone are the tremolos and dry accents, the discords and caesuras—there is instead a graduated melody that plays through the varying tonal intensity of the line. From these works in which the typical formula often prevails over the obstinate search for characterization derives that aspect of Modigliani's graphic *oeuvre* that makes his last period, undeservedly, the best known and the most appreciated by the public. It is also the most counterfeited.

But alongside this subtle abandonment to more mannered and accessible cadences there appears a new invention of style: the development, that is, of what was originally Cézanne's architectural structure (having passed through the abstract purism of Brancusi, the asymmetry of primitive and African art, the distortions of the Cubists) into a spontaneous and natural fusion of reality and formal harmony. The line runs firmly and lightly in defining the features of the model, without strain or abstract distortion; a coherent artistic idiom is completely merged with the physical and emotional depiction of the subject. A higher serenity dissolving in melancholy, a resigned nostalgia for beauty animate these figures modeled in a soft essence of light. The "return to order," so much in the air at the time, finds in these drawings a lyrical solution, an intimate accord between art and nature. There are, of course, lapses into decorative arabesques and intellectualizing formulas, and often the model's facial and emotional traits are accentuated. But there are many masterpieces to show how these three tendencies, present from the beginning in Modigliani's art, found in this period their most limpid unity. These are the many portraits of Jeanne Hébuterne (Plate 82), Lunia Czechowska (Plates 80, 91, 92), Zborowski, Donato Frisia (Plate 71), Bernouard, Mondzain (Plate 72), Hayden (Plate 75), Mario

Varvogli (Plate 94)—figures absorbed in dreams, in secret evocations translated by the artist into the fluent rhythms of musical lines and soft, supple forms. Each individual, with his burden of passions and experience, has now become a living caryatid in the Temple of Beauty.

"A great work of art should be considered as any other work of nature," wrote the young Modigliani in 1901. In these last drawings he succeeded in combining art, the study of form, and human passion in a natural flowering of Style.

# BIOGRAPHICAL OUTLINE

1884 Amedeo Clemente Modigliani born July 12 in Livorno (Leghorn), Italy.

1895 Attends the *liceo* (secondary school) in Livorno. Falls ill with a severe case of pleurisy.

1898 After recovering from an attack of typhus, begins to study art with Guglielmo Micheli in Livorno.

1901 After an attack of tuberculosis, he is sent on a tour of convalescence to Capri; visits Naples, Rome, and Florence.

1902 Enrolls in the Scuola Libera di Nudo of the Accademia di Belle Arti, Florence.

1903 Enrolls at the Istituto di Belle Arti, Venice.

1906 Moves to Paris at the beginning of the year, where he attends art classes at the Colarossi school. Becomes friendly with Maurice Utrillo, meets Max Jacob, André Salmon, Guillaume Apollinaire, and Picasso.

1907 Becomes acquainted with Dr. Paul Alexandre, who makes the first purchases of paintings and drawings from him.

1908 First exhibition: five paintings and a drawing in the Salon des Indépendants.

1909 Meets Juan Gris and becomes friendly with Brancusi. Begins to work in sculpture. Returns to Livorno for a few months in the summer.

1910 Returns to Paris. Exhibits six paintings in the Salon des Indépendants.

1912 Exhibits seven sculptures in the Salon d'Automne.

1914 Becomes acquainted with Beatrice Hastings, and with the Polish poet and art dealer Leopold Zborowski. Makes his first sales to Paul Guillaume.

1917 Meets Jeanne Hébuterne, with whom he moves into a studio in the Rue de la Grande Chaumière. First one-man show, at the Galerie Berthe Weill, organized by Zborowski.

1918 Sojourn in Nice and Cannes. On November 29, his daughter Jeanne is born.

1919 Very ill, he returns to Paris in May. Exhibition in the Hill Gallery, London, and in the Salon d'Automne. Jeanne Hébuterne is expecting their second child.

1920 Modigliani dies at the Hôpital de la Charité, Paris, on January 24. Jeanne commits suicide on January 25.

1907

Modigliani
all'amico Bucci

4

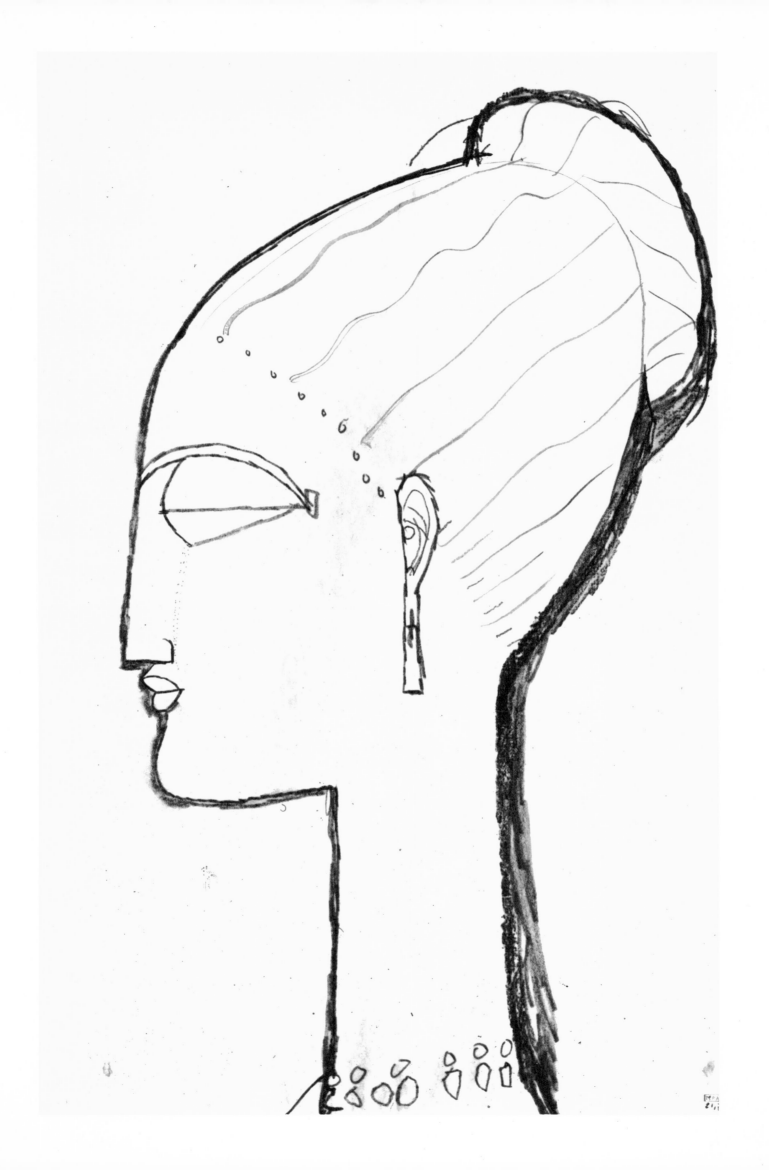

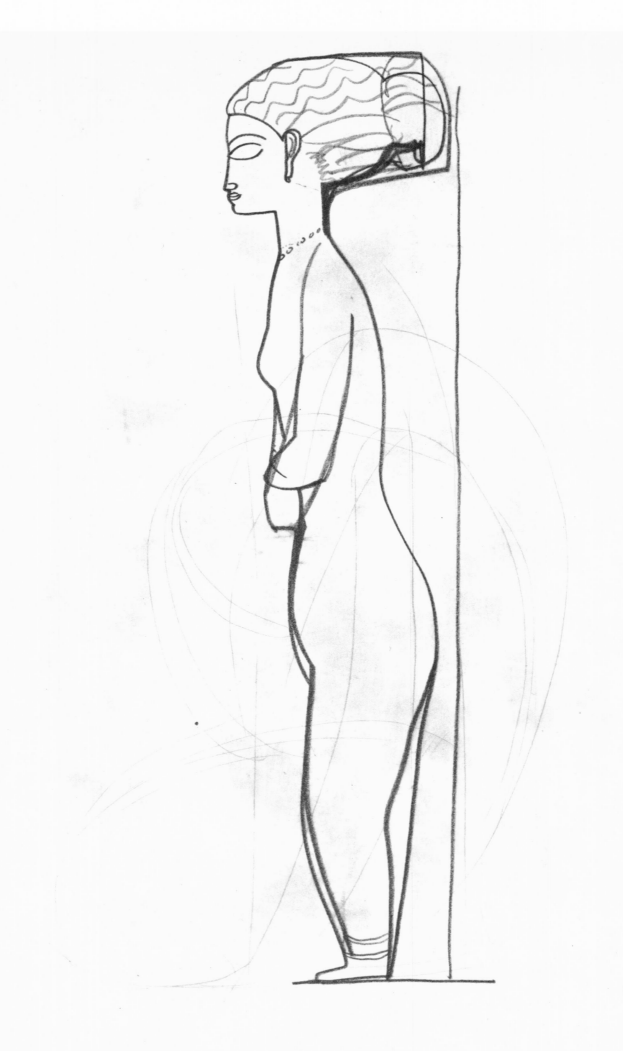

9

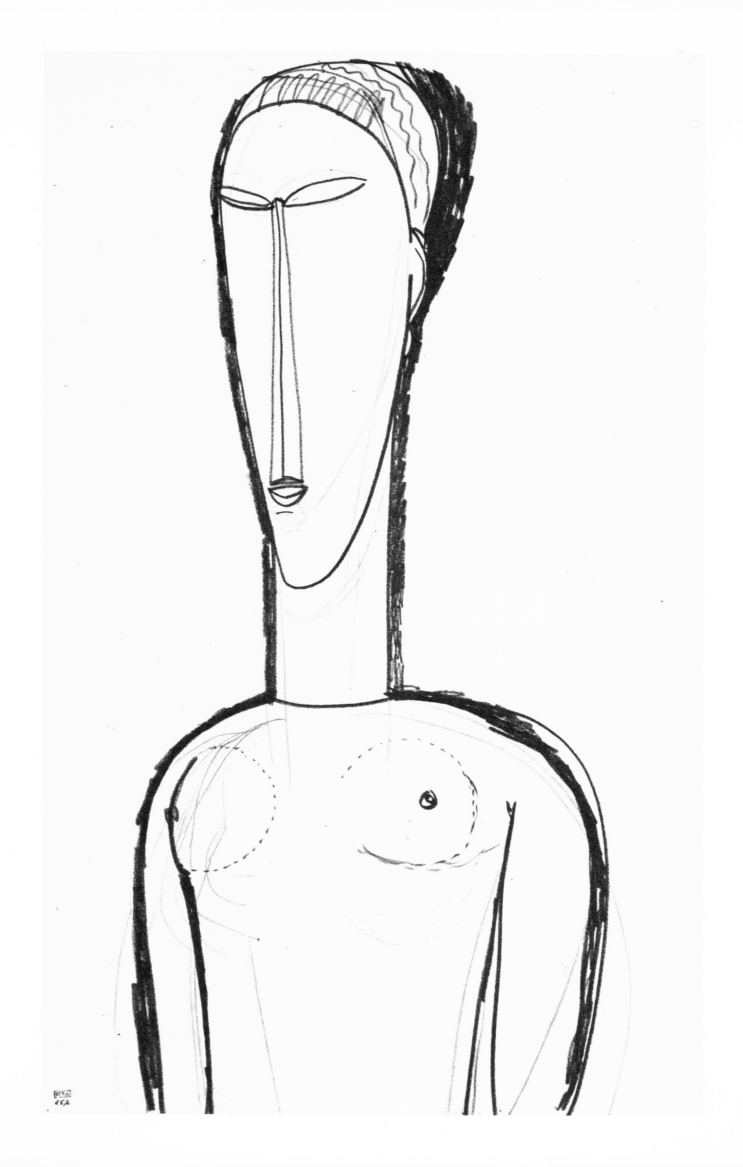

20

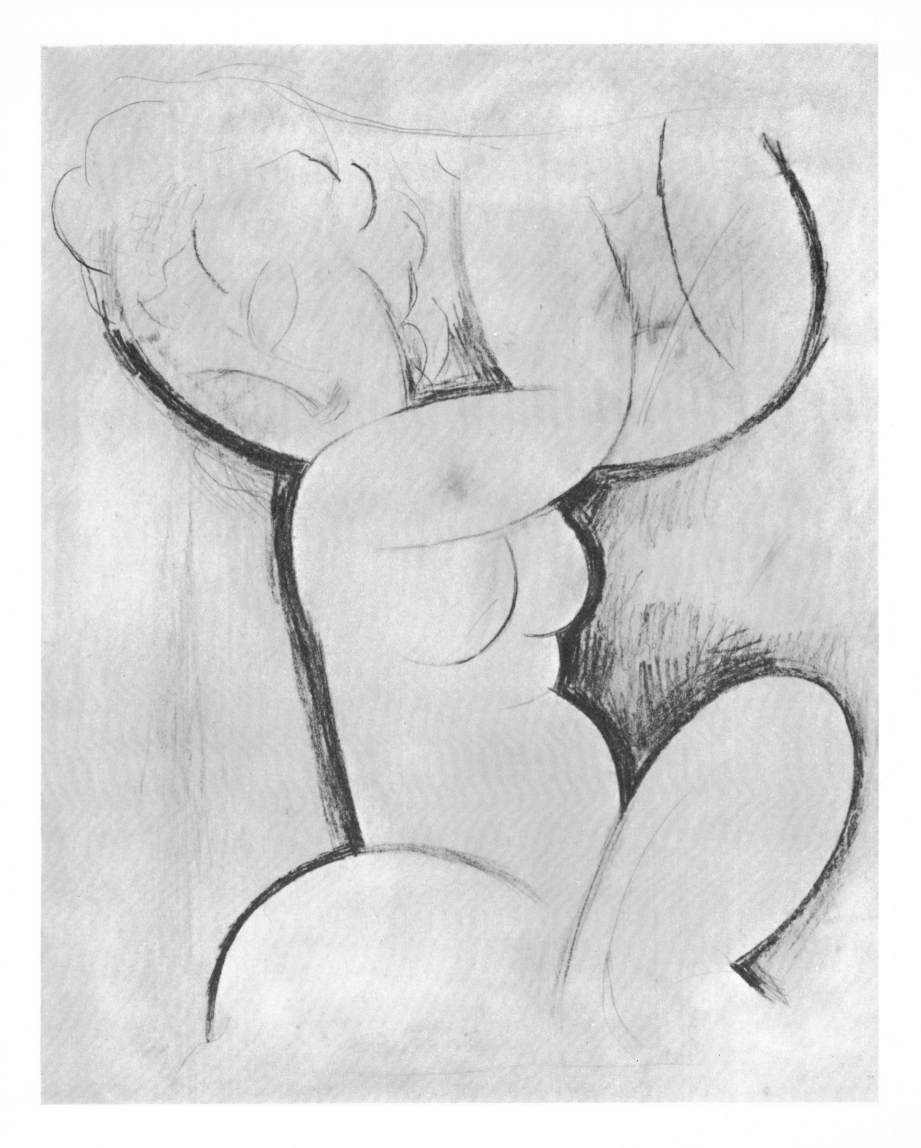

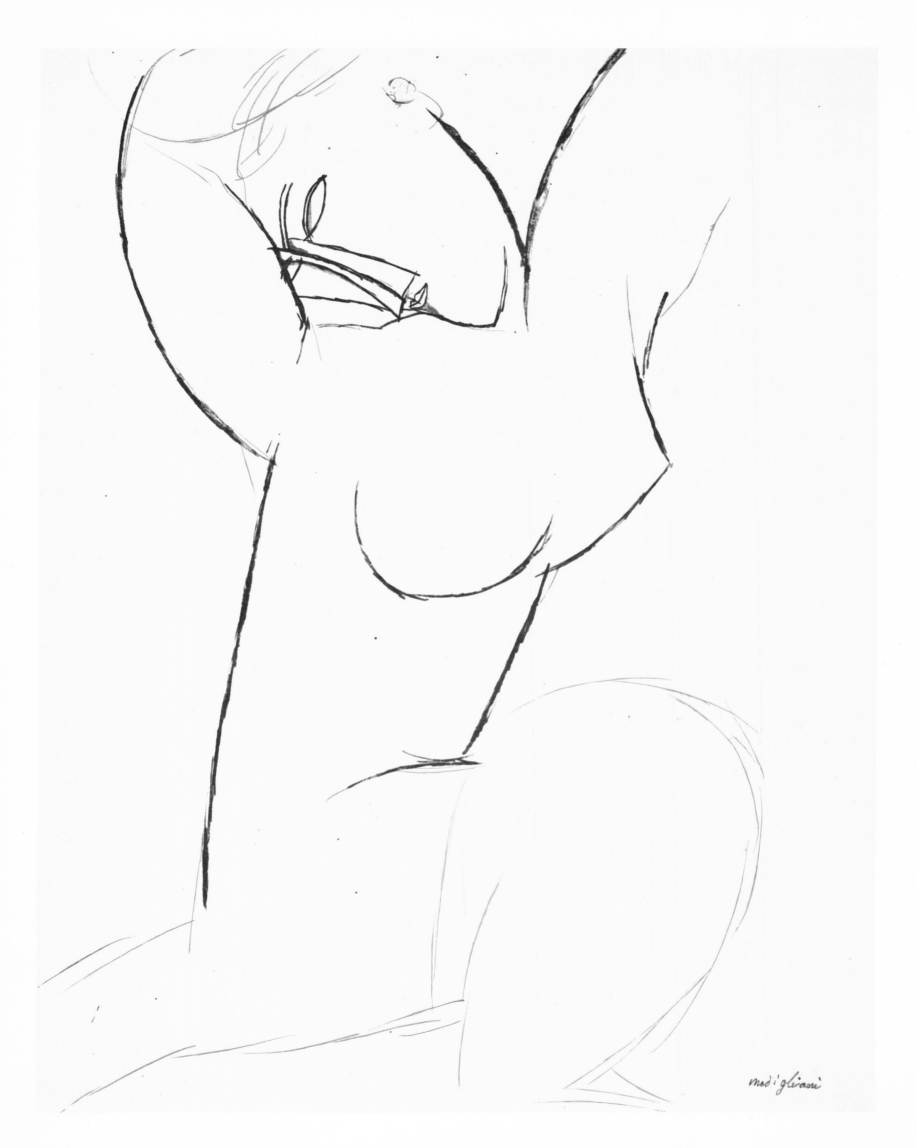

23

Sourds drames nocturnes..
Féeries nocturnes
Escarbouclées!
Jusqu'à ce que jaillissent
en les féeriques palais,
engés,
les avalanches de lumière
en les féeriques palais
engés.
sur des Colonnes de lumière

Ricercari soleva biondi e branchi e di vita
dorse
e nel primo fiore —

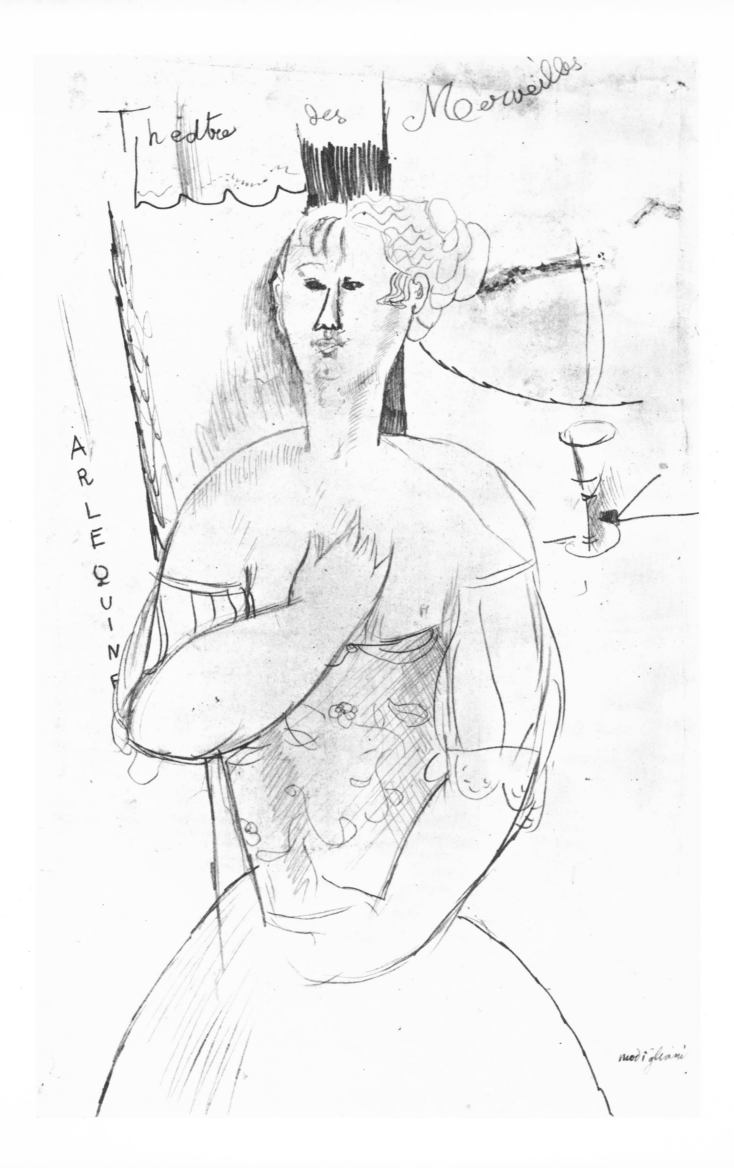

32

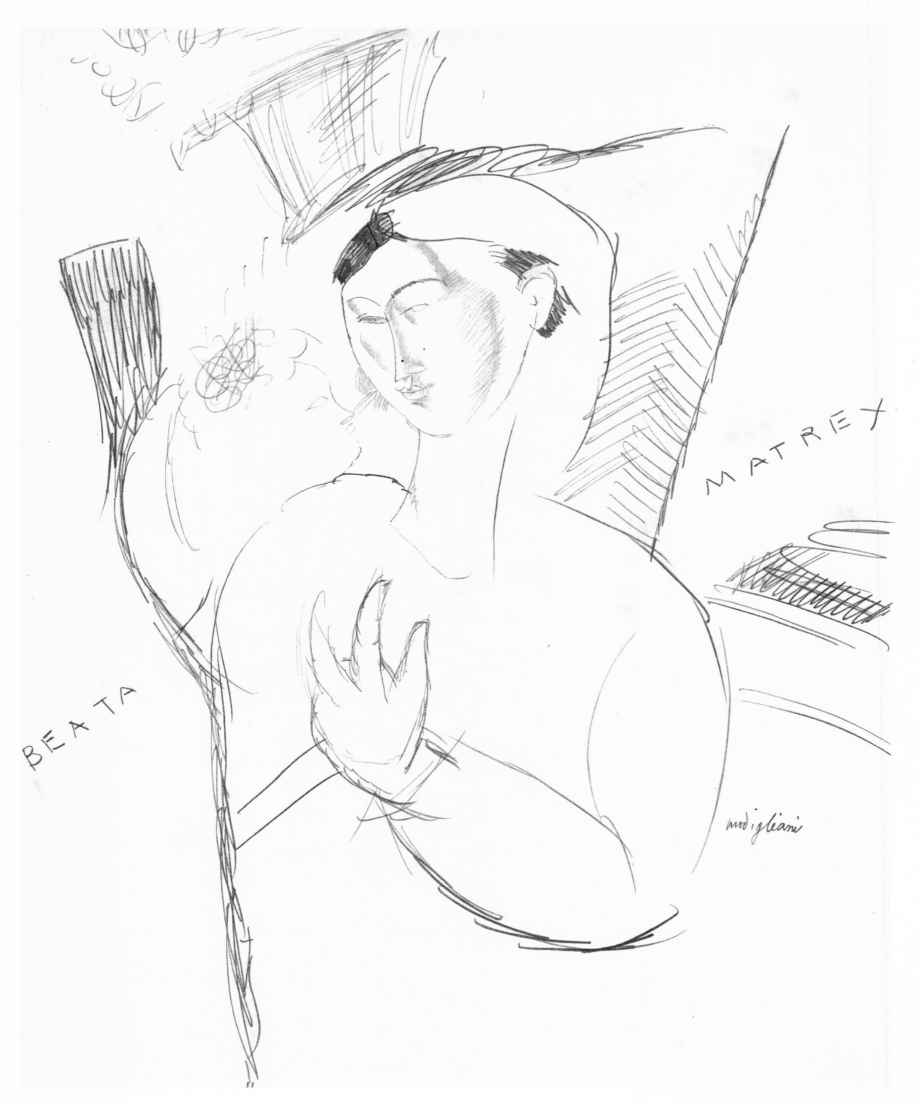

BEATA

MATREX

modigliani

33

Les deux Orphelines.

15

modigliani

34

35

LA VITA
DOMESTICA

S
A
N
T
A

SOEUR CHARITABLE

1915

Parigi modigliani

modigliani

modigliani

modigliani

modigliani

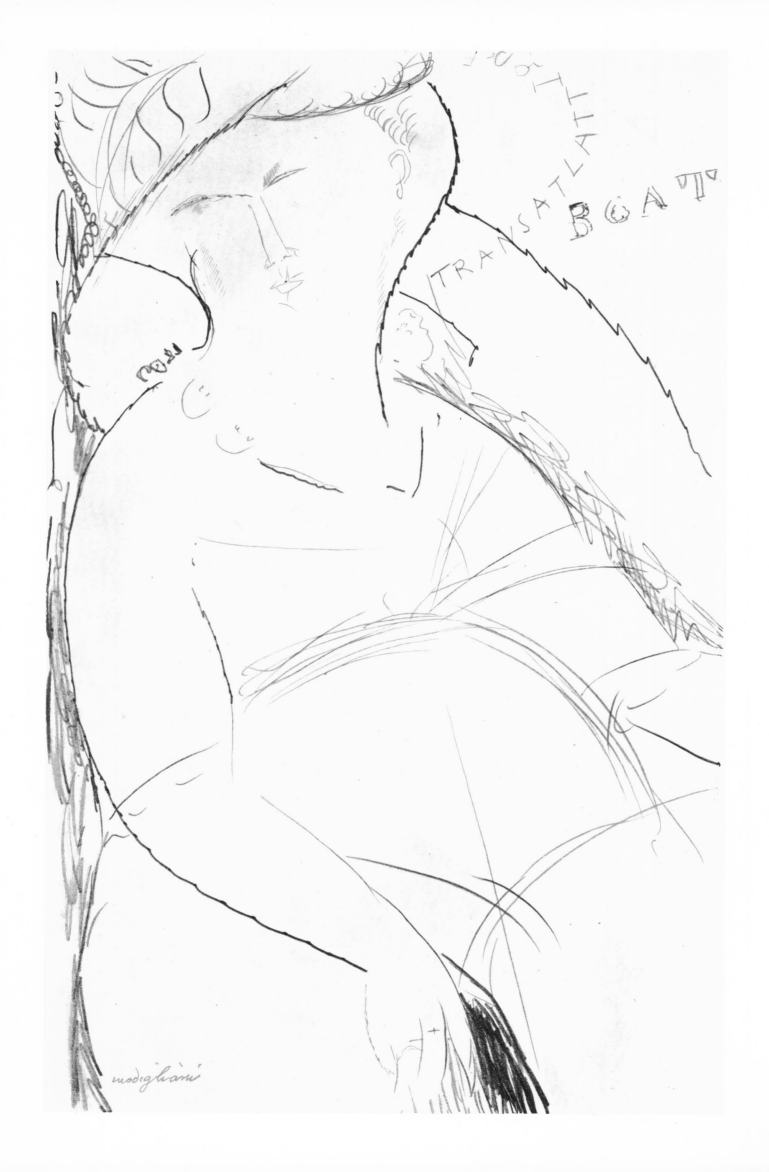

modigliani

modigliani

45

ANADIOMENA

MODIGLINAI

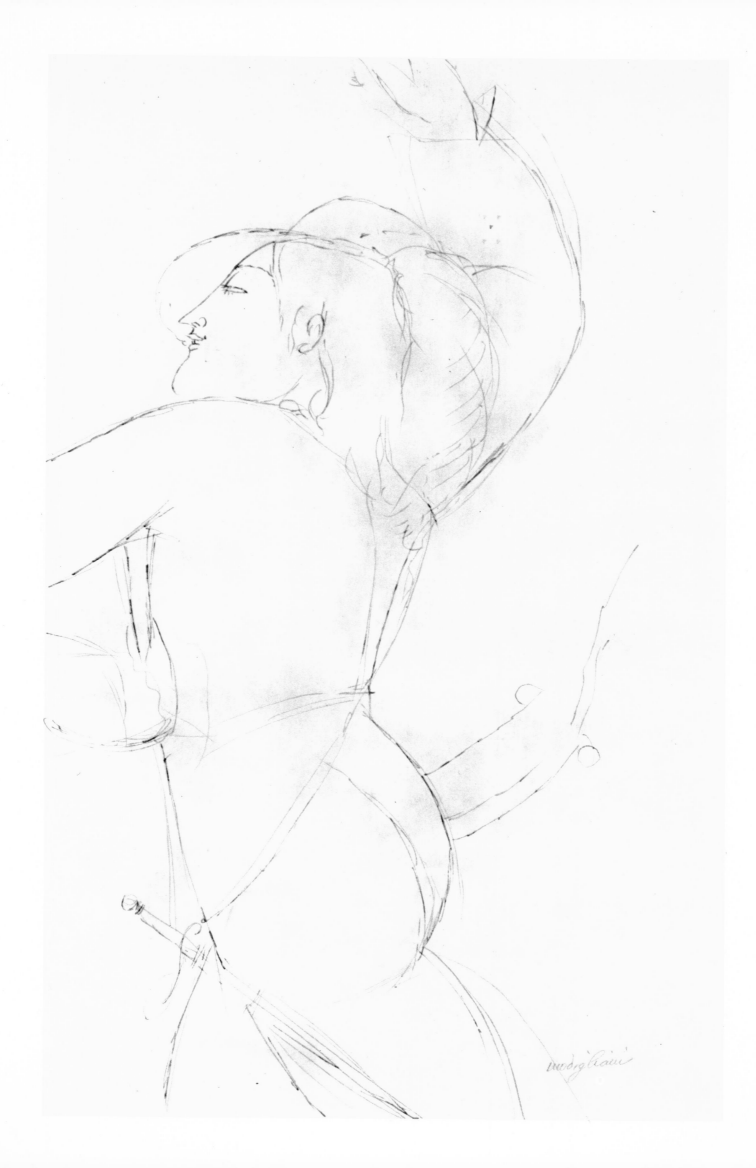

modigliani

51

LIPCHITZ

PAUL GUILLAUME

modigliani.

53

modigliani

à

CHABAN IAN-HERAN

1916

modigliani

56

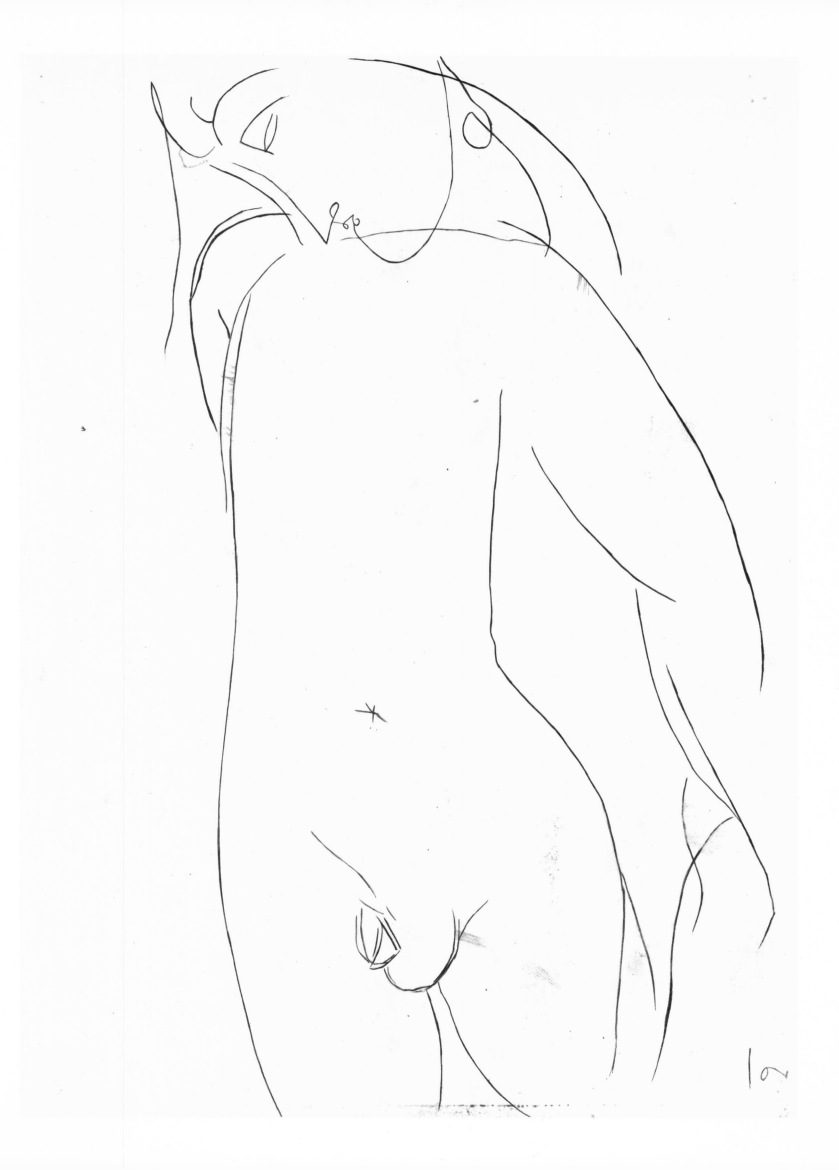

à Mademoiselle
Jadine.

Portrait de Derain                                    modigliani

à Dermée

Modigliani

à Guerin.
le 11 Novembre.
1919
modigliani.

modigliani

modigliani

№ 2 gieleni. 20 Nov 1919

Sventura volle che in Donna de... di Desserti insiem
Si grande Animo e di Si Ornato...
Andissela una ismisurato...
Fioco

84

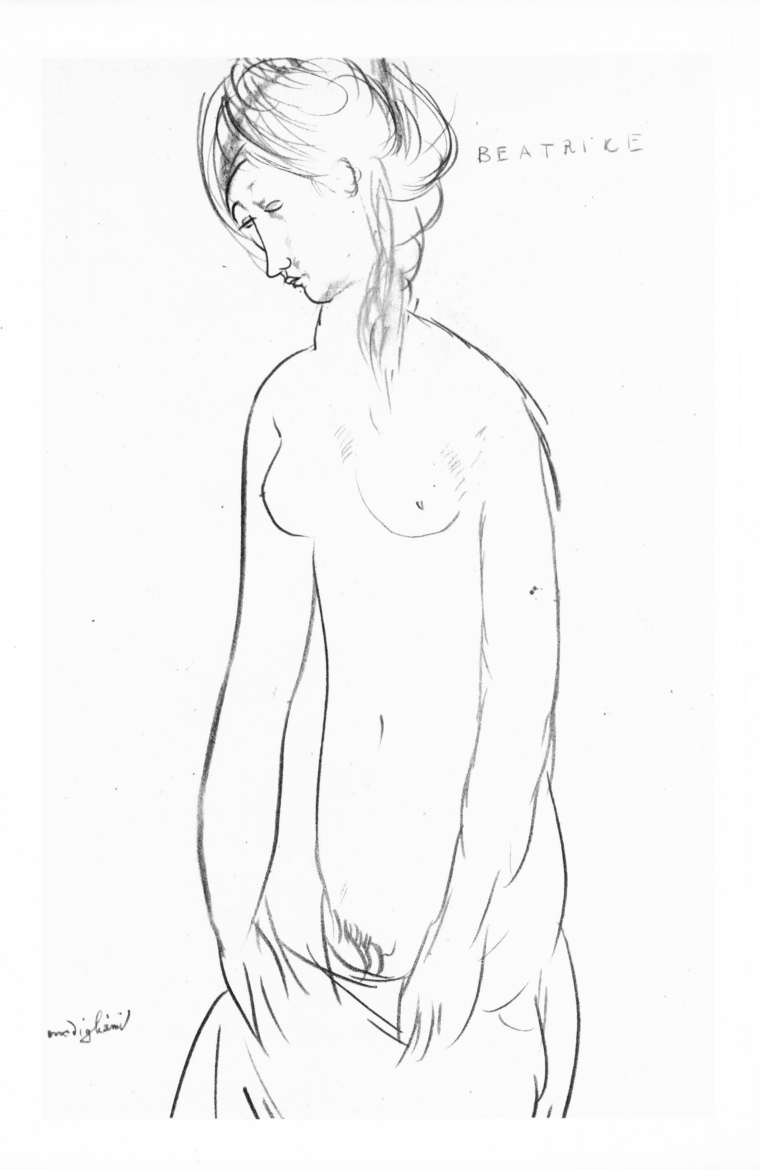

BEATRICE

modigliani

Modigliani

hommage
à
Madame Chakoska.
modigliani

Dimensions of the drawings are always given height first, followed by width. The bibliographic citations (for example: Bibl. 3) are to the General Bibliography of this volume.

Colorplate following page VI:

*Nude*

Pencil and watercolor, 21¹/₄ × 16⁷/₈″. Signed lower right. c. 1913/14. Private collection, Rome.

Bibl. 3 (Plates 32, 33), Bibl. 37 (Plate 4), Bibl. 55, Bibl. 57 (No. 61), Bibl. 66 (No. 49).

In the catalogue of the 1959 Rome exhibit (Bibl. 66), Nello Ponente indicated the kinship of this drawing with the painting *Seated Nude* in the Courtauld Institute, London. Its date is 1912/13, thus somewhat earlier than the one here. The classical motif shows influences of Ingres and Puvis de Chavannes and recalls drawings by Picasso on the same theme. Stylistically the drawing could have been done in 1914, while the painting in the Courtauld Institute is probably a repetition of the same theme and seems to have been executed later, after 1916. One might also compare with both drawing and painting the *Nudes* which Modigliani executed in 1917 (reprod. in Bibl. 78, p. 192), inspired by Puvis de Chavannes' painting *L'Espérance*. The drawing shown here may also be considered related to the *Nude* shown in Bibl. 7 (Plate 25).

Colorplate following page X:

*Caryatid*

Pastel and crayon with brush strokes, 20⁷/₈ × 19″. Signed lower right. c. 1913/15. Musée du Petit Palais, Collection Girardin, Paris.

Bibl. 42 (No. 46), Bibl. 57 (No. 51), Bibl. 59 (No. 39), Bibl. 63 (No. 259), Bibl. 66 (No. 51), Bibl. 83 (p. 105, Plate 9).

In the rotation of the *figura serpentinata* relationships with manneristic sculptural motifs become evident; they are taken up again in the style of Art Nouveau and at the same time point to African sculpture. In addition to a series of caryatid studies, Modigliani varied the posture of the human body in dynamically curved compositions (cf. Plates 118, 127, 130 in Bibl. 6).

Colorplate following page XIV:

*Portrait of Pablo Picasso*

Oil on cardboard, 13³/₈ × 10¹/₄″. Signed lower left, and inscribed above: "Picasso," below: "Savoir." c. 1915. Collection Georges Moos, Geneva.

Bibl. 6 (Plate 51), Bibl. 19, Bibl. 22 (p. 38), Bibl. 39 (p. 88), Bibl. 41, Bibl. 42, Bibl. 43, Bibl. 57 (No. 13), Bibl. 60 (p. 22), Bibl. 64 (No. 20), Bibl. 66 (No. 8).

One could call this a colored drawing rather than an oil painting. The drafting and graphic organization, arabesques, and sculptural structure mark and characterize this beautiful picture. (Cf. also Plate 46.)

Colorplate following page XVIII:

*Rosa Porprina*

Crayon and oil on cardboard, 17³/₈ × 10⁵/₈″. Signed lower left, and dated lower right: "16 Feb. 1915—Paris." Inscribed above: "Rosa Porprina." Collection Dr. Riccardo Jucker, Milan.

Bibl. 6 (Plate 52), Bibl. 13 (Plate 53/1954), Bibl. 19 (Plate 66), Bibl. 37 (Plate 12), Bibl. 42 (No. 51), Bibl. 53 (No. 16), Bibl. 56 (No. 26), Bibl. 57 (No. 58), Bibl. 60 (p. 27, 1954; p. 29), Bibl. 71 (Plate XIII), Bibl. 82 (p. 76), Bibl. 86 (p. 99), Bibl. 88 (Plate 11).

In 1915, besides a drawing in a private collection in Milan and the portrait of Madame Friesz (*La Marseillaise,* cf. Bibl. 7, Plate 132), Modigliani several times used and varied similar techniques. We are dealing with drawings on cardboard with oils contributing accents. They portray extended and soft forms whose outlines are accentuated by colored speckles and dots. Compare, for example, with the portraits of Picasso and Rivera (Colorplate following p. XIV and Plate 45) various portraits of Beatrice Hastings (reprod. in Bibl. 39, p. 28), paintings and drawings like *Portrait of a Woman* in the Collection Castaing, Paris (Bibl. 66, No. 55), *Teresa,* formerly Collection Dutilleul, Paris (Bibl. 48, No. 8), *Mateo* in the Collection H. Pearlman, New York (Bibl. 60, p. 27), among others.

## BLACK-AND-WHITE PLATES

1   *Head of a Woman with Hat*

Watercolor, 13³/₄ × 10⁵/₈″. Signed lower left. c. 1907/8. Collection Sidney F. Brody, Los Angeles, California.

Bibl. 7 (Plate 2).

Cf. the painting *Nude with Hat,* Collection P. Alexandre (reprod. in Bibl. 7, Plate 4).

2   *Bust of a Woman*

Watercolor, 12 × 9″. Signed lower right. c. 1907/8. Private collection, U.S.A.

Bibl. 7 (Plate 3), Bibl. 18 (p. 34).

Like the preceding drawing, this one uses the same model as *Nude with Hat* and *The Jewess.*

3   *Portrait of Mario Buggelli*

Pencil, 13 × 9⁷/₈″. Signed at center bottom and dedicated: "all'amico Bucci." 1907. Property of the heirs of Anselmo Bucci, Monza.

Bibl. 37 (Plate 1), Bibl. 57 (No. 59), Bibl. 66 (No. 58).

Mario Buggelli, author and art critic, and Anselmo Bucci, author, painter, and engraver, belonged to the group of Italian artists Modigliani often met with during the early days of his Paris residence. Bucci left interesting memoirs of the period and his meeting with Modigliani.

4   *Portrait of Kohler*
India ink. Signed lower left and dedicated: "à Kohler bien amicale-ment." c. 1908/9. Private collection, U.S.A.
Bibl. 15 (Plate 80).
Compare with the drawing reprod. in Bibl. 7 (Plate 7), which uses the same model.

5   *Head of a Woman in Profile with Earrings*
Pen, $7^1/_4 \times 4^5/_8$″. Signed lower left. c. 1913/14. Collection Pierre Gran-ville, Paris.
Bibl. 48 (No. 45), Bibl. 49 (No. 227), Bibl. 57 (No. 73), Bibl. 64 (No. 169), Bibl. 66 (No. 65), Bibl. 67 (No. 19), Bibl. 82 (p. 78).

6   *Head of a Woman in Profile with Earrings*
Pencil, $16^3/_4 \times 10^1/_2$″. Lower right stamp of the Collection Dr. P. A. n. 21,7. c. 1910/11. Hanover Gallery, London.
Bibl. 7 (Plate 57), Bibl. 52 (No. 7), Bibl. 86 (p. 103).

7   *Standing Nude in Profile*
Pencil, $16^7/_8 \times 10^1/_4$″. Lower right stamp of the Collection Dr. P. A. n. 21,8. c. 1910/11. Private collection, Paris.
Bibl. 7 (Plate 53).
One of a series of studies for the sculpture *Standing Nude* in the Collec-tion Gustave Schindler, New York.

8   *Head of a Woman in Profile with Earrings*
Pencil, $16^3/_4 \times 10^1/_2$″. Lower left stamp of the Collection Dr. P. A. n. 19,9. c. 1910/11. M. Knoedler & Co., Inc., New York.
Bibl. 7 (Plate 44).
As in Plate 6, this is a study for a sculpture. Characteristics related to the *Head* reprod. in Bibl. 7 (Plate IX, Plate 47); present owner unknown.

9   *Head of a Woman, Front View, with Earrings*
Pencil, $16^7/_8 \times 10^1/_2$″. Lower right stamp of the Collection Dr. P. A. n. 30. c. 1910/11. Berggruen & Cie., Paris.
Bibl. 7 (Plate 56).
Study for a sculpture.

10   *Standing Nude in Profile*
Pencil, $16^7/_8 \times 8^5/_8$″. Lower right stamp of the Collection Dr. P. A. n. 20,1. c. 1910/11. Berggruen & Cie., Paris.
Bibl. 7 (Plate 94), Bibl. 48 (No. 36).
Study for the sculpture *Standing Nude* in the Collection Gustave Schind-ler, New York.

11   *Head of a Woman, Front View*
Blue pencil, $13^3/_8 \times 10^1/_2$″. Lower right stamp of the Collection Dr. P. A. n. 21,4. c. 1910/11. Berggruen & Cie., Paris.
Bibl. 7 (Plate 83).
Study for the sculpture *Head* in the Philadelphia Museum of Art, Philadelphia, Pennsylvania.

12   *Portrait of a Woman, Three-quarter View*
Pencil, $16^7/_8 \times 10^1/_4$″. Lower left stamp of the Collection Dr. P. A. n. 25,2. c. 1910/11. Berggruen & Cie., Paris.
Bibl. 7 (Plate 99).
Study for a sculpture.

13   *Caryatid*
Pencil, $14^7/_8 \times 10^1/_8$″. Not signed. c. 1910/12. Collection Pierre Gran-ville, Paris.
Bibl. 37 (Plate 3), Bibl. 48 (No. 39), Bibl. 49 (No. 225), Bibl. 57 (No. 63), Bibl. 64 (No. 165), Bibl. 66 (No. 62), Bibl. 67 (No. 6).
Study for a sculpture.

14   *Caryatid*
Pencil, $16^7/_8 \times 10^1/_2$″. Lower right stamp of the Collection Dr. P. A. n. 32. c. 1910/12. Berggruen & Cie., Paris.
Bibl. 7 (Plate 108).
Study for a sculpture. In the background, upper right, there is a menorah, a symbol which is particularly interesting here as the fusion of a classical motif (the caryatid) with a Hebraic one.

15   *Seated Nude*
Blue pencil, $16^7/_8 \times 10^1/_2$″. Lower left stamp of the Collection Dr. P. A. n. 3,37. c. 1910/11. Berggruen & Cie., Paris.
Bibl. 7 (Plate 20).

16   *Standing Nude in Profile*
Blue pencil, $16^7/_8 \times 10^1/_2$″. Lower right stamp of the Collection Dr. P. A. n. 3,40. c. 1910/11. Collection Max Ponder, U.S.A.
Bibl. 7 (Plate 19), Bibl. 48 (No. 35).

17   *Kneeling Nude*
Mauve chalk, $16^7/_8 \times 10^1/_4$″. Signed lower right. c. 1910/11. Berg-gruen & Cie., Paris.
Bibl. 7 (Plate 15), Bibl. 48 (No. 37).

18   *Study with African Sculpture and Caryatid*
Pencil, $10^1/_2 \times 8^1/_8$″. Signed lower right. c. 1912/13. Collection James W. Alsdorf, Winnetka, Illinois.
Bibl. 38 (Plate 61), Bibl. 39 (Plate 67), Bibl. 42 (No. 50), Bibl. 46 (No. 2), Bibl. 53 (No. 53/i), Bibl. 58 (p. 88), Bibl. 83 (p. 98).

19   *Caryatid*
Pencil, $10^5/_8 \times 8^1/_4$″. Not signed. c. 1913/14. Private collection, Flor-ence.
One of a series of drawings, watercolors, and pastels of which the best known are in the collection of Mrs. Sydney G. Biddle, West Chester (reprod. Bibl. 7, Plate 117) and the Norton Gallery, West Palm Beach, Florida (reprod. Bibl. 38, Plate 75). Compare also Bibl. 83 (pp. 108–9). The reproduction shown in Bibl. 38 (Plate 79) shows the greatest simi-larity with this drawing.

20   *Caryatid*
Pencil, $10^5/_8 \times 8^1/_4$″. Not signed. c. 1913/14. Private collection, Flor-ence.
One of a series of studies, most important of which is the drawing with the inscription "Opulentia," formerly in the Collection Zborowski (reprod. in Bibl. 25 and there dated 1916).

21   *Caryatid*
Blue pencil, $28 \times 22^7/_8$″. Not signed. c. 1914/15. The Philadelphia Museum of Art, Louise and Walter Arensberg Collection, Philadelphia, Pennsylvania.
Bibl. 13 (p. 29), Bibl. 38 (Plate 62), Bibl. 48 (No. 41).

22   *Caryatid*
Blue pencil, $28 \times 22^7/_8$″. Signed lower right. c. 1914/15. The Phila-delphia Museum of Art, Louise and Walter Arensberg Collection, Philadelphia, Pennsylvania.
Bibl. 38 (Plate 69), Bibl. 48 (No. 42).

23   *Study for a Caryatid*
Ink and pencil, $21^5/_8 \times 16^1/_2$″. Signed lower right. c. 1913. Collection Sforni, Como.
Bibl. 4 (unpaged), Bibl. 6 (pp. 12, 70), Bibl. 56 (No. 21), Bibl. 83 (p. 111). One of a group of sketches for caryatid sculptures. The presentation of the figure is similar to that of the sculpture in the Museum of Mod-

ern Art, New York. Compare also the reproductions in Bibl. 20 (Plate 3), and Bibl. 38 (Plate 83); also, with reference to the stylistic similarity with the drawings illustrated in Bibl. 37 (Plates 5, 7).

24 *Study for a Caryatid*
Ink and pencil. Signed lower right. c. 1913. Private collection.
Stylistically related to the preceding drawing. Compare the representation of the head with the sculpture in a private collection in Paris reproduced in Bibl. 38 (Plates 54, 55).

25 *Portrait of a Seated Man*
Pencil, 16$^1$/$_2$ × 9$^7$/$_8$″. Signed lower right. c. 1915/16. Musée National d'Art Moderne, Paris.
Bibl. 12 (Plate 24), Bibl. 20 (Plate 18).

26 *Head of a Woman*
Pencil and red crayon, 10$^1$/$_2$ × 7$^7$/$_8$″. Not signed. c. 1910/13. Hanover Gallery, London (formerly Collection Arthur Pfannstiel).
Bibl. 18 (p. 42), Bibl. 20 (Plate 5), Bibl. 38 (Plate 57).
Study for a sculpture; compare particularly with the *Head* in the Tate Gallery, London.

27 *Seated Nude*
Pencil, 21$^1$/$_2$ × 16$^7$/$_8$″. Signed lower right. c. 1913/15. Collection Lamberto Vitali, Milan.
Bibl. 37 (Plate 7), Bibl. 42, Bibl. 56, Bibl. 57.

28 *Seated Woman*
Pencil, 16$^1$/$_8$ × 9$^7$/$_8$″. Signed lower right. c. 1915. Collection Dr. Emilio Jesi, Milan.
Bibl. 57.
Stylistically related to paintings like *La Jolie Ménagère* (Barnes Foundation, Merion, Pennsylvania) and *La Petite Louise* (Private collection, Paris).

29 *Circus Acrobat*
Pencil, 20$^1$/$_2$ × 14$^5$/$_8$″. Not signed. Inscription: "Livorno. Sours drames nocturnes. Féeries nocturnes, Escarbouclées. Jusqu'à ce que jaillissent en les féeriques palais érigés, les avalanchesde lumière, en les féeriques palais érigés, sur des colonnes de lumière." Below, in blue pencil: "Ricercarli soleva biondi e bianchi e di vita destra e nel primo fiore." c. 1914. Formerly Galerie Marcel Bernheim, Paris.
Bibl. 39 (Plate 64, p. 48), Bibl. 57 (No. 71), Bibl. 59 (No. 78), Bibl. 64, Bibl. 66 (No. 66), Bibl. 67 (No. 8).
There are many drawings on which Modigliani wrote verses, quotations, or remarks. This drawing is related to *La Dompteuse* (Collection M. Lewis, Alliance, U.S.A.), *Harlequin* (formerly Galerie Marcel Bernheim, Paris, reprod. in Bibl. 39, Plates 54, 55), and Plate 30 of this catalogue.

30 *Dancer*
Pencil, 17$^3$/$_8$ × 10$^5$/$_8$″. Signed lower right. c. 1914. The Art Museum, Princeton University, Princeton, New Jersey.

31 *Couple*
Pen and brush in ink, 8$^1$/$_2$ × 6$^1$/$_2$″. Signed upper right. c. 1914. Collection James W. Alsdorf, Winnetka, Illinois.
Bibl. 20 (Plate 9), Bibl. 42, Bibl. 46 (No. 13).
This is probably the first version of the "Bride and Groom" motif—in the same style as the preceding Plates 29 and 30—which, influenced by Cubism, was subsequently further developed in the watercolor *Le Ménage* in the Sidney F. Brody Collection, Los Angeles (cf. Bibl. 7, Plate 133), and in the famous painting *Bride and Groom* in the Museum of Modern Art, New York.

32 *Portrait of a Woman*
Pencil, 16$^1$/$_2$ × 9$^1$/$_2$″. Signed lower right, and inscribed: "Théatre des Merveilles" (above) and "Arlequine" (left center, vertical). c. 1915. Collection Frank Stoop, London.
Bibl. 18 (p. 38), Bibl. 20 (Plate 7), Bibl. 54 (No. 76).
Similar to the drawing *Seated Harlequin,* formerly Collection Silvio Gabriolo, Milan, reprod. in Bibl. 37 (Plate 9).

33 *Beata Matrex*
Pencil, 21$^1$/$_4$ × 16$^1$/$_2$″. Signed right, and inscribed: "Beata Matrex." c. 1915. Collection Lamberto Vitali, Milan.
Bibl. 37 (Plate 20), Bibl. 51, Bibl. 56 (No. 40), Bibl. 57 (No. 80).

34 *The Two Orphans*
Pencil, 16$^3$/$_4$ × 10$^3$/$_8$″. Signed lower right; inscription upper left: "Les deux Orphelines." c. 1916. Collection Stefa and Leon Brillouin, New York.
Bibl. 45 (No. 16).
There are several known drawings by Modigliani representing two persons or a couple. Besides the above Plate 31, the following drawings may be mentioned: Bibl. 7 (Plates 133 and 146), Bibl. 45 (Nos. 14 and 18), *Au Bar* (Bibl. 18, p. 57), *Adam and Eve* in the Collection Dr. Emilio Jesi, Milan, and others. The drawing illustrated here is particularly similar to the one in a private collection in Milan (cf. Bibl. 74, p. 484), which is also assumed to be a study for the *Portrait of Jacques Lipchitz and His Wife* in the Art Institute of Chicago. Lipchitz, however, disagrees with this identification (cf. Bibl. 45, p. 25).

35 *Beatrice Hastings in an Armchair*
Pencil, 16$^1$/$_2$ × 10$^1$/$_4$″. Signed lower right. c. 1915. Collection Dr. Giuseppe Vismara, Milan.
Bibl. 37 (Plate 16), Bibl. 57 (No. 88).
Modigliani made several sketches of this composition. The one most similar to this one is illustrated in Bibl. 45 (No. 15).

36 *Domestic Life*
Pencil. Signed lower right, and inscribed: "La vita domestica," "Santa," "Soeure Charitable," and (above the signature) "Parigi." Lower left the date 1915. Formerly Collection Huguette Berès, Paris.
This is a portrait of Beatrice Hastings similar to the previous illustration.

37 *Portrait of Beatrice Hastings*
Pencil, 7$^1$/$_8$ × 4$^3$/$_8$″. Signed lower left. c. 1915/16. Collection Gianni Mattioli, Milan.
Bibl. 6 (p. 35), Bibl. 17 (p. 17), Bibl. 23 (Plate 3, p. 17), Bibl. 37 (Plate 13), Bibl. 42 (No. 62), Bibl. 57 (No. 93), Bibl. 70 (No. XI), Bibl. 79 (No. 107), Bibl. 86 (No. 66).
One of Modigliani's most famous drawings of his mistress Beatrice Hastings, an English poetess.

38 *Seated Woman*
Pencil, 15$^3$/$_8$ × 9$^7$/$_8$″. Not signed. c. 1915/16. Collection Mrs. Paul H. Sampliner, New York.
Bibl. 37 (Plate 26), Bibl. 57 (No. 83), Bibl. 60 (Frontispiece in the 1951 edition), Bibl. 66 (No. 49).
As Agnes Mongan noted, this drawing may be compared with two others in the Brillouin Collection (Bibl. 45, Nos. 8, 9).

39 *Seated Young Man, Full Face*
Pencil, 16$^3$/$_4$ × 10$^1$/$_4$″. Signed lower left. c. 1915. Kunstmuseum, Basel.
Bibl. 37 (Plate 24), Bibl. 57 (No. 75), Bibl. 66 (No. 72).
A further study of this same portrait follows in Plate 40. Both drawings correspond stylistically with Plate 32.

40 *Seated Young Man, Full Face*
Pencil, 16³/₄ × 10¹/₂″. Not signed. c. 1915. Private collection.
Compare Plate 39.

41 *Seated Woman*
Pencil, 16⁷/₈ × 10¹/₄″. Signed lower left. c. 1914/15. Collection Giorgio Soavi, Milan.
This drawing shows quick, inventive strokes, as well as a sculptural organization. It may therefore be compared with the *Portrait of Diego Rivera* (Plate 45) and *Woman with Hat* (Plate 42).

42 *Woman with Hat*
Pencil, 16³/₄ × 10¹/₈″. Signed lower left. c. 1915. Collection Prof. Antonio Morassi, Milan.
Bibl. 56 (No. 28), Bibl. 57 (No. 78), Bibl. 66 (No. 74).
Compare the note to Plate 41.

43 *The Passenger—"Transatlantique Boat"*
Pencil, 16¹/₂ × 10¹/₄″. Signed lower left, and inscribed: "Transatlattique [sic] Boat." c. 1915. Collection Mr. and Mrs. James W. Alsdorf, Winnetka, Illinois.
Bibl. 20 (Plate 6), Bibl. 39 (Plate 65, p. 48), Bibl. 42 (No. 63), Bibl. 46 (No. 25), Bibl. 58 (p. 91).
Probably the same as Plates 41, 42, and 44, or at least stylistically related to these drawings.

44 *Seated Woman in an Armchair*
Pencil, 16¹/₂ × 10¹/₈″. Signed lower left, and inscribed: "LA." Kunstmuseum, Basel.
Bibl. 57 (No. 87), Bibl. 66 (No. 79).
Shows the same stylistic characteristics as the previous drawings, Plates 39-43.

45 *Portrait of Diego Rivera*
Pencil, 13⁵/₈ × 8³/₄″. Signed left, and inscribed upper right: "Rivera." c. 1914. Collection Michel Grilichess, Paris.
Bibl. 20 (Plate 12), Bibl. 24 (Plate 3, p. 4), Bibl. 37 (Plate 8), Bibl. 42 (No. 55), Bibl. 48 (No. 46), Bibl. 57 (No. 70), Bibl. 59 (No. 46), Bibl. 64 (No. 164), Bibl. 66 (No. 69), Bibl. 76 (p. 95), Bibl. 82 (p. 78), Bibl. 87 (Plate 26).
Modigliani did at least two portraits of the Mexican painter Diego Rivera in oil on cardboard (cf. Bibl. 6, Plates 31 and 32) as well as several drawings, of which the one presented here is the best known.

46 *Portrait of Pablo Picasso*
Pencil, 8¹/₄ × 9⁷/₈″. Not signed. c. 1915. Collection Renée Laporte, Paris.
Bibl. 22 (p. 39), Bibl. 31 (Plate 40), Bibl. 48 (No. 49), Bibl. 59 (No. 55), Bibl. 64 (No. 156), Bibl. 66 (No. 68), Bibl. 67 (No. 17).
Besides this drawing and the one in oil on paper (Colorplate following p. XIV) there is another one of 1915 showing Picasso with cap and pipe It is in the Musée National d'Art Moderne in Paris and comes out of a sketchbook (reprod. in *Art de France*, 1964, p. 371). A third drawing may possibly also be a picture of Picasso (Collection H.P. Roché, Paris; cf. Bibl. 64, No. 178, and Bibl. 67, No. 53).

47 *Anadiomena*
Pencil and yellow crayon, 13³/₈ × 10¹/₂″. Signed lower right; left vertical inscription: "Anadiomena." c. 1914/15. The Art Museum, Princeton University, Princeton, New Jersey.
This drawing, which continues the development of the caryatid motif, may be grouped stylistically with Plates 41-44. From 1914 on motifs taken from Greek mythology frequently appear in Modigliani's drawings.

48 *Man in the Costume of a Dancing Musketeer*
Pencil and pen, 16⁵/₈ × 10¹/₄″. Signed lower right. c. 1914/15. The Art Museum, Princeton University, Princeton, New Jersey.
This drawing, which probably refers to a ballet scene or a stage play, may be compared with other pictures from the same period (e.g. Bibl. 57, No. 92).

49 *Seated Nude*
Pencil, 19¹/₈ × 13³/₈″. Signed lower right. c. 1915/16. Private collection.
One may assume that this nude study still belongs to a period in which Modigliani was more concerned with sculpture. A new blend of archaic symbols and the influence of African sculpture and Cubism shows itself. The naturalistic movements of the body are mostly dissolved. This drawing should probably be dated the same as those in Bibl. 45 (No. 21), Bibl. 46 (No. 6), and Bibl. 20 (No. 52).

50 *Portrait of a Young Girl*
Pencil, 10 × 7⁷/₈″. Signed lower left. c. 1916. Collection Mrs. Donald Ogden Stewart, London.
The drawing is probably a portrait of Beatrice Hastings.

51 *Portrait of Max Jacob*
Pencil, 11 × 8⁵/₈″. Not signed; inscribed: "Max Jacob." c. 1916. Collection Luciano Pomini, Castellanza.
Bibl. 7 (Plate 142), Bibl. 20 (Plate 24), Bibl. 50 (No. 59), Bibl. 57 (No. 76), Bibl. 59 (No. 60), Bibl. 66 (No. 70).
Modigliani did many drawings and oil portraits of his great friend Max Jacob, the poet and painter. One should here recall a painting formerly in the possession of the Pierre Roché Collection, Paris, now in the Cincinnati Museum, and another, dated 1916, formerly in the Lefèvre Collection and now in the Museum in Düsseldorf. There are two drawings that have certain similarities with the painting in the Roché Collection. One, No. 213 in the 1967 catalogue, is in the Hannema-De Stuers Foundation in Nijenhuis Castle in Heino, Holland; the other, in a private collection, was published in my article (cf. Bibl. 85). Up to now it has not been possible to identify the model.

52 *Portrait of Jacques Lipchitz*
Pencil, 11³/₄ × 9⁷/₈″. Not signed; inscribed upper right: "Lipchitz." c. 1916. Musée de Peinture et de Sculpture, Grenoble.
Bibl. 75 (No. 157).
In 1916 Modigliani painted a portrait of Lipchitz and his wife (today in the Art Institute of Chicago). Max Jacob had introduced Lipchitz to Modigliani in 1913. In his book dedicated to Modigliani Lipchitz recalls that the former did "a number of preliminary drawings, one right after the other, with impressive speed and precision." One should compare with the drawing here, left to the Museum in Grenoble by the Sarmiento Foundation, the two illustrations in Bibl. 18 (p. 74) and Bibl. 13 (ed. Garzanti, p. 3) in which the figure is presented three-quarter face.

53 *Portrait of Paul Guillaume*
Pencil, 21¹/₄ × 16⁷/₈″. Signed lower left; upper vertical inscription: "Paul Guillaume." c. 1916. Collection Jacques Dubourg, Paris.
Bibl. 20 (Plate 27), Bibl. 37 (Plate 21), Bibl. 44 (No. 141), Bibl. 48 (No. 50), Bibl. 49 (No. 234), Bibl. 57 (No. 91), Bibl. 59 (No. 68), Bibl. 64 (No. 157), Bibl. 66 (No. 82).
Modigliani made the acquaintance of Paul Guillaume through Max Jacob in 1914. Guillaume encouraged him in his work and acquired several examples of it. There is a series of portraits of him—drawings and oils—produced between 1915 and 1916. The four best-known paintings are reproduced in Bibl. 6 (Plates 55, 56, 58, 62). Besides the drawing illustrated here is the portrait in the Brillouin Collection (Bibl. 45, No. 12) and two heads (Bibl. 15, Plates 82, 83).

54 *Portrait of Chadanian-Heran*
Pencil, $16^7/_8 \times 10^1/_4''$. Signed lower left, and dedicated: "Modigliani à Chadanian-Heran." c. 1916. Present owner unknown.
It is most difficult to date drawings like this one. Given the freedom and artistic power of the facial expression, it might be considered to have been done within Modigliani's final period. However, considering the structure of the masses, achieved by varying the density of the strokes, it may refer back to the stylistic characteristics of the period between 1916 and 1917.

55 *Portrait of Madame Kisling*
Pencil, $16^1/_8 \times 10^1/_4''$. Signed lower left. c. 1916. Collection Mrs. Renée Kisling, Sanary-sur-Mer.
Bibl. 37 (Plate 28), Bibl. 57 (No. 96), Bibl. 59 (No. 50), Bibl. 64 (No. 173), Bibl. 66 (No. 86).
The painter Moïse Kisling and his wife Renée were among the closest of Modigliani's friends and frequently posed for him. In Kisling's studio on the rue Joseph Bara, Modigliani painted some of his most famous works. In addition to this drawing I recall at least two portraits in oil depicting Renée Kisling, painted respectively in 1916 and 1917. The latter is in the National Gallery of Art, Washington, D.C. (Chester Dale Collection), and the former, in a private collection, is reproduced in Bibl. 20a, Plate 22.

56 *Portrait*
Pen and watercolor, $12^7/_8 \times 9^3/_4''$. Signed lower right. c. 1916. Collection Robert von Hirsch, Basel.
This sketch can be compared with paintings like, for example, *Fillette à la chevelure* (Bibl. 7, Plate 165), and with drawings like the one presumed to be of Beatrice Hastings (cf. Bibl. 20, Plate 26).

57 *Resting Male Nude*
Pen and blue pencil, $10^1/_4 \times 13^3/_8''$. Signed lower right. Collection Georges Moos, Geneva.
This drawing, with its classically mannerist motif, which may be noted also in the sculpture studies of the same period, was probably done in 1914/15.

58 *Standing Male Nude*
Pen, $13 \times 9^1/_4''$. Not signed. Private collection, Paris.
Bibl. 24 (p. 475).
Like the preceding drawing, this one, too, may be dated 1914/15. Compare also the *Nude* reprod. in Bibl. 15 (Plate 98).

59 *Purgatorius Animus*
Pencil, $17^1/_8 \times 10^5/_8''$. Signed lower right, and inscribed: "Purgatorius" (above) and "Animae" (left). c. 1916/18. Private collection, Como.
Bibl. 23 (Plate p. 32), Bibl. 56 (No. 46).
From 1915 on many of Modigliani's drawings were on religious themes with corresponding inscriptions. From *Christ Crucified* (Collection Gio Ponti, Milan) to the numerous studies of figures in prayer (cf. the plates in Bibl. 45, Nos. 14, and 18-20, and Bibl. 57, Nos. 98, 99, 106, 113), these motifs occupied Modigliani for two years. One may guess that the choice of this theme was not a little influenced by Max Jacob, who converted to Catholicism. The drawing illustrated here is particularly closely related to another, *Dies Irae, Dies Illae*, reproduced in Bibl. 36 (Plate 19).

60 *Nude Praying*
Pencil, $11^3/_4 \times 8^5/_8''$. Signed lower left. c. 1917. Private collection, Milan.
Bibl. 56, Bibl. 57 (No. 113), Bibl. 66 (No. 105).
Compare the note to Plate 59.

61 *Seated Woman*
Pencil, $18^1/_8 \times 10^1/_4''$. Signed lower left. c. 1917/18. Collection Gianni Mattioli, Milan.
Bibl. 6 (Plate p. 31), Bibl. 42 (No. 81), Bibl. 48 (No. 61), Bibl. 57 (No. 125), Bibl. 68 (No. 65), Bibl. 70 (Plate XIII).
As Agnes Mongan noted (cf. Bibl. 45, p. 31), this drawing shows the same model in the same pose as Plate 29 in the catalogue of the Brillouin Collection. We may agree with this assumption, since we are probably dealing here with two studies for a portrait of the sculptress Chana Orloff.

62 *Standing Nude, Full Face*
Pencil, $15^3/_8 \times 9^1/_2''$. Signed lower right. c. 1917/18. Private collection, Milan.
Bibl. 37 (Plate 37), Bibl. 56, Bibl. 57 (No. 130), Bibl. 66 (No. 121).
The harmony of its formal structure and the liveliness of its facial expression make this drawing one of the most noteworthy of the numerous nude studies.

63 *Portrait of a Woman*
Pencil, $18^7/_8 \times 12^1/_4''$. Signed lower right. c. 1916. Collection Robert J. Sainsbury, London.
Bibl. 3 (Plate 37), Bibl. 24 (Plate 4, p. 4), Bibl. 37 (Plate 27), Bibl. 57 (No. 105), Bibl. 66 (No. 94).
This is probably a portrait of Mme. Zborowska.

64 *Mademoiselle Jachine*
Pencil, $10^5/_8 \times 8^1/_4''$. Not signed. Dedication lower right: "à Mademoiselle Jachine." c. 1917. Collection Mme. R. Hein, Paris.
Bibl. 20 (Plate 37), Bibl. 44 (No. 140), Bibl. 57 (No. 111), Bibl. 59 (No. 59), Bibl. 66 (No. 101).
Mademoiselle Jachine, later Mme. Hein, was a friend of Jeanne Hébuterne and with her attended the École des Arts Décoratifs where Modigliani met her.

65 *Portrait of a Man with Hat*
Pencil, $12^5/_8 \times 9''$. Signed lower right. Inscribed lower left in a strange hand: "Portrait de Derain." c. 1916. Musée de Peinture et de Sculpture, Grenoble.
Bibl. 72 (p. 207), Bibl. 75 (No. 160).
As G. Viatte remarked in his note on this drawing (cf. Bibl. 75), the inscription identifying the model of this portrait is not in Modigliani's hand, and the similarity with the French painter's features is not established. A portrait drawn by Modigliani does exist (Collection Mme. Derain, cf. Bibl. 59, No. 51). Viatte also indicates the similarity of this drawing with the figure of the bridegroom in the painting *Bride and Groom* (Museum of Modern Art, New York). Compare also Plate 76.

66 *Portrait of Paul Dermée*
Pencil, $13 \times 9^7/_8''$. Signed lower left, and dedicated: "à Dermée." c. 1917/19. Musée de Peinture et de Sculpture, Grenoble.
Bibl. 75 (No. 161).
Paul Dermée, poet, critic, and art dealer, founded the magazine *Nord-Sud* in 1917 and *L'Esprit Nouveau* in 1921.

67 *Portrait of Charles Guérin*
Pencil, $16^3/_4 \times 10^3/_8''$. Signed lower right, and dedicated: "à Guérin. le 11 Novembre 1919." The Museum of Modern Art, New York, Gift of John S. Newberry in honor of Paul J. Sachs.
Charles Guérin (1875-1939), painter and author, was highly regarded by Guillaume Apollinaire. Since this beautiful drawing was dated by Modigliani, we have a dependable stylistic criterion for his final period.

68 *Portrait of Gillet*
Pencil, $10^5/_8 \times 8^1/_4''$. Signed lower left, and dedicated: "à Gillet."
c. 1917/19. Musée de Peinture et de Sculpture, Grenoble.
Bibl. 75 (No. 159).
G. Viatte (cf. Bibl. 75) thinks this drawing does not definitely represent
Louis Gillet but perhaps one of the artists of the same name who
visited Montparnasse at that time: the painters Eugène and Numa
François or the sculptor Lucien Gillet.

69 *Portrait of René Durey*
Pencil, $18^7/_8 \times 15^3/_4''$. Not signed. c. 1917/19. Collection Dr. Emilio
Jesi, Milan.
Bibl. 7 (Plate 143).
The painter Durey, also a friend of Gabriel Fournier, who drew a
portrait of him in 1917 (cf. Bibl. 71, p. 136), was a regular visitor to
Montparnasse and painted many pictures of that section.

70 *Portrait of Sola*
Pencil, $16^5/_8 \times 10''$. Signed upper right, and inscribed: "Sola." c. 1918/
1919. Collection Mme. Huguette Berès, Paris.
Bibl. 86 (p. 100).
In the drawings of Modigliani's last years the lines are scattered and
light, in great curves, without however losing their plastic strength.

71 *Portrait of Donato Frisia*
Pencil, $17^1/_8 \times 10^1/_2''$. Not signed. c. 1919. Collection Dr. Emilio Jesi,
Milan.
Bibl. 56 (No. 61), Bibl. 57 (No. 120), Bibl. 77 (p. 50).
Modigliani drew several portraits of his friend, the Lombard painter
Donato Frisia (1883-1953). Compare besides the drawing illustrated
here the reproductions in Bibl. 3 (Plates 44-46), and Bibl. 37 (Plate 39).

72 *Portrait of Simon Mondzain*
Pencil, $18^7/_8 \times 11^3/_8''$. Signed upper right, and dedicated: "Multa
Renascentur à Mondzain." c. 1918/19. Collection Simon Mondzain,
Paris.
Bibl. 48 (No. 63), Bibl. 72 (p. 126).
Mondzain came to Paris in 1910 together with his friend Kisling,
through whom he probably met Modigliani.

73 *Portrait of a Man with Hat*
Pen, $10^3/_8 \times 7^7/_8''$. Signed lower left. c. 1917/18. The Abrams Family
Collection, New York.
Bibl. 23 (Plate 7, p. 29), Bibl. 39 (Plate 62, p. 47), Bibl. 67 (No. 45).
A beautiful example of concentration on the essential in Modigliani's
art. Physiognomy and accessories are united by the composition.

74 *Portrait of Conrad Moricand*
Pen, $10^1/_2 \times 8^1/_4''$. Not signed. c. 1916/17. Private collection.
Conrad Moricand (1887-1954), author and artist, was a close friend of
Modigliani's. There is another drawing of him by Modigliani (cf. Bibl.
45, No. 13). Agnes Mongan in her note to this drawing reminds us
that it was Moricand who, together with Kisling, tried to obtain a
death mask of Modigliani but with poor results, so that Lipchitz had
to put the broken pieces of the plaster cast back together again and
make the final impression.

75 *Portrait of the Painter Henri Hayden*
Pencil, $16^1/_8 \times 9^7/_8''$. Signed lower middle. Left vertical inscription:
"Hayden." c. 1919. Collection Gianni Mattioli, Milan.
Bibl. 7 (Plate 152), Bibl. 23 (Plate 6, p. 24), Bibl. 42 (No. 88), Bibl. 56
(No. 51), Bibl. 57 (No. 126), Bibl. 59 (No. 43), Bibl. 68 (No. 68), Bibl.
70 (cover), Bibl. 79 (Plate 108).

76 *Portrait of André Derain*
Pencil, $21^1/_4 \times 11^3/_8''$. Not signed. 1918/19. Collection Mme. André
Derain, Paris.
Bibl. 31 (Plate 39), Bibl. 59 (No. 51), Bibl. 67 (No. 63).
Compare note to Plate 65. Modigliani also did a portrait of the artist's
wife, Alice.

77 *Portrait of Gilanc*
Pencil, $21^1/_4 \times 14^1/_8''$. Signed lower right. Right vertical inscription:
"No. 2 Gilanc—20 Nov. 1919." Berggruen & Cie., Paris.
This drawing, done a few days after the portrait of Charles Guérin
(Plate 67), shows in comparison the security and freedom with which
Modigliani increasingly worked out the various expressions of his
style. One should note here the echoes of symbols and formulas he
developed during his sculptural period between 1914 and 1916.

78 *Portrait of a Man*
India ink, $13 \times 9^7/_8''$. Signed upper right. c. 1918/19. Collection Gianni
Mattioli, Milan.
Bibl. 7 (Plate 151), Bibl. 18 (p. 75), Bibl. 37 (Plate 35), Bibl. 42 (No. 90),
Bibl. 56 (No. 53), Bibl. 57 (No. 124), Bibl. 68 (No. 67), Bibl. 70 (Plate
XIV), Bibl. 79 (Plate 110).

79 *Portrait of a Woman*
Pencil, $16^1/_2 \times 9^7/_8''$. Not signed. c. 1918. Collection Lord Sandwich.
Bibl. 86 (p. 104).

80 *Woman with Hat*
Pencil, $10^5/_8 \times 8^1/_4''$. Signed below. c. 1918/19. Collection Prof. Candido
Mantelli, Turin.
Bibl. 37 (Plate 42), Bibl. 56 (No. 58), Bibl. 57 (No. 137), Bibl. 66 (No.
127).
This drawing may be a portrait of Mme. Lunia Czechowska, a close
friend of Modigliani and Jeanne Hébuterne. From 1916 to 1919 Modigliani did many portraits of Mme. Czechowska, whom he had met
through Zborowski.

81 *Portrait of a Woman with Hat*
Pencil, $19^3/_8 \times 11^7/_8''$. Signed lower left. c. 1918/19. The Museum of
Modern Art, New York.
Bibl. 7 (Plate 150), Bibl. 10 (Plate 16), Bibl. 15 (Plate 85/1958, Plate
90/1962), Bibl. 23 (Plate 9), Bibl. 40 (No. 39), Bibl. 47 (No. 43), Bibl.
60 (No. 53).

82 *Portrait of Jeanne Hébuterne*
Pencil, $13 \times 9^7/_8''$. Signed lower left. c. 1919. Collection Pierre Gran-
ville, Paris.
Bibl. 6 (Plate p. 27), Bibl. 37 (Plate 45), Bibl. 48 (No. 60), Bibl. 49 (No.
231), Bibl. 57 (No. 117), Bibl. 59 (No. 64), Bibl. 64 (No. 168), Bibl. 66
(No. 110), Bibl. 67 (No. 55).
This is certainly the most beautiful of the many portraits Modigliani
did of his companion Jeanne Hébuterne.

83 *Portrait of Mrs. Arthur Cravan*
Pencil and blue pencil, $19^1/_4 \times 12''$. Not signed. c. 1918/19. The Art
Museum, Princeton University, Princeton, New Jersey.
It is claimed in an article that this drawing is a portrait of the wife of
Arthur Cravan, one of the most colorful personalities in Montparnasse
from 1913 to 1915. He was a poet and a boxer and claimed to be Irish
and a nephew of Oscar Wilde. In 1914 an exhaustive article by him
appeared in the magazine *Maintenant* and created quite a scandal. In
1916 he challenged the world boxing champion Jack Johnson, who
scored an immediate knockout in the ring. At the invitation of Marcel
Duchamp, Cravan gave a lecture in New York in 1917 in honor of the

first exhibition of "independent American artists." During the lecture he tried a striptease, but the police intervened. He seems to have married Mina Loy, a young Englishwoman, who followed him to Mexico, where he disappeared shortly thereafter. We are not sure whether Mina Loy-Cravan returned to France after 1917, as must have been the case if this drawing, which certainly dates from 1918/19, really is a portrait of her.

84  *Portrait of a Woman with Hat*
Pencil, 12³/₈ × 11⁵/₈″. Not signed. Inscribed below: "Sventura volle che in Donna di sì Grande Animo e di sì Ornato Sapere Ardesse uno ismisurato Fuoco di Desideri Insani." c. 1917/18. The Art Museum, Princeton University, Princeton, New Jersey.
It is very difficult to identify this model. There are certain similarities with photographs of Jeanne Hébuterne but also with others of Modigliani's models.

85  *Beatrice*
Pencil, 15⁷/₈ × 10″. Signed lower left, and inscribed upper right: "Beatrice." c. 1916/18. Collection Georges Renand, Paris.
Bibl. 3 (Plate 42), Bibl. 7 (Plate 131), Bibl. 10 (1951, Plate 59), Bibl. 12 (Plate 12), Bibl. 20 (Plate 31), Bibl. 36 (1929, Plate 5), Bibl. 37 (Plate 33), Bibl. 57 (No. 134), Bibl. 59 (No. 72), Bibl. 64, Bibl. 66 (No. 125), Bibl. 80 (p. 44).
This drawing is generally assumed to be a nude of Beatrice Hastings and was therefore dated 1915 by Ceroni (Bibl. 7); however, as Vitali (Bibl. 36) and Pfannstiel (Bibl. 20) have noted, it has certain characteristics of the period around 1918. The nude must therefore either have been drawn from memory or be of Jeanne Hébuterne and simply called Beatrice with D'Annunzian wit.

86  *Bust of Jeanne Hébuterne or Lunia Czechowska in Profile*
Pencil, 13¹/₂ × 11″. Signed lower right. c. 1919. Kunstmuseum, Basel.
Bibl. 20 (Plate 49), Bibl. 24 (Plate 1), Bibl. 57 (No. 135), Bibl. 66 (No. 126).
This beautiful drawing is reminiscent of the famous portrait of Lunia Czechowska in profile, reproduced in Bibl. 6 (Plate 148), although the model's hairstyle, with bangs over the forehead, is different.

87  *Reclining Nude*
Pencil, 11³/₄ × 18¹/₈″. Signed lower right. c. 1918. Collection Pierre Granville, Paris.
Bibl. 20 (Plates 28, 29), Bibl. 48 (No. 66), Bibl. 49 (No. 230), Bibl. 57 (No. 139), Bibl. 64 (No. 167), Bibl. 66 (No. 129).

88  *Standing Nude with Right Leg Drawn Up*
Pencil, 15¹/₂ × 10″. Signed lower left. c. 1918/19. Collection Dr. Emilio Jesi, Milan.
Bibl. 37 (Plate 43), Bibl. 56 (No. 59), Bibl. 57 (No. 136).
This drawing is probably one of a series after the same model, two of which are reproduced in Bibl. 3 (Plates 48 and 49).

89  *Seated Girl, Front View*
Pencil, 16⁷/₈ × 10⁵/₈″. Signed lower left. c. 1917. Collection Dr. Emilio Jesi, Milan.
Bibl. 37 (Plate 30), Bibl. 56, Bibl. 57 (No. 103).

90  *Seated Woman with Arms Crossed*
Pencil, 16¹/₂ × 9⁷/₈″. Not signed. Inscribed lower left: "male"(?). c. 1918. Collection Jean Lenthal, Paris.
Bibl. 18 (p. 71), Bibl. 20 (Plate 41), Bibl. 36 (Plate 8).
Probably Lunia Czechowska.

91  *Portrait of Lunia Czechowska*
Pencil. Signed lower right, and inscribed upper right: "La Vita é un Dono: dei pochi ai molti: di Coloro che Sanno e che hanno a Coloro che non Sanno e che non hanno." c. 1919. Private collection.
Bibl. 18 (p. 64).
In her memoirs, published in Ceroni (Bibl. 6), Lunia Czechowska tells how this drawing was done one evening by candlelight in Zborowski's house while she was preparing dinner (cf. Bibl. 6, p. 32). Corrado Maltese in his article (cf. Bibl. 76) identifies the source of the inscription: it is a remark made by D'Annunzio and published in *Convito* in 1895 (Vol. I, 29). Also compare this drawing with the painting in the Collection H. J. Heinz (Bibl. 6, Plate 145).

92  *Hommage à Madame Chekoska*
Pencil, 12⁵/₈ × 9¹/₂″. Signed lower left, and dedicated: "Hommage à Madame Chekoska [sic]." c. 1919. Collection Robert von Hirsch, Basel.
Bibl. 18 (p. 67), Bibl. 20 (Plate 33), Bibl. 31 (Plate 48), Bibl. 41 (No. 96), Bibl. 43 (No. 117), Bibl. 61, Bibl. 62.
Together with the two preceding plates and another shown in Bibl. 7 (Plate 154), this is one of the most beautiful and carefully executed drawings Modigliani did of Lunia Czechowska.

93  *Seated Young Woman*
Pencil, 20¹/₂ × 14¹/₈″. Signed lower right. c. 1919. Collection Galerie Berggruen & Cie., Paris.
The drawing is a pendent to the *Portrait of Gilanc* (Plate 77).

94  *Portrait of Mario Varvogli*
Pencil. Signed lower right. c. 1919. Private collection.
Bibl. 12 (Plate 36), Bibl. 25.
This is the most carefully worked out study of all and comes closest to the famous painting in the Meyer Collection, Zurich (cf. Bibl. 6, Plate 153). The Greek musician Mario Varvogli disclosed in a letter of April 28, 1959, that Modigliani did the first sketch for his portrait in 1917 and that the artist wrote on it the same phrase which appears on the portrait of Lunia Czechowska (Plate 91). As Maestro Varvogli recalls, the portrait was painted in three sittings some months after Modigliani's return from Nice, that is, the end of 1919, and remains unfinished. Varvogli did not meet Modigliani again and only heard of his death from friends who took him to the station when he had to leave suddenly for Athens to take up his teaching duties at the Conservatory. The other known drawing is in the Museum of Modern Art, New York (cf. Bibl. 7, Plate 156), and carries the inscription "Il Nuovo Anno— Hic Incipit Vita Nuova." It may have been done during the same sitting and in the same pose on January 1, 1920. As the drawing of the sculptor Antonios Sochos published by me in my article (Bibl. 84) proves, Modigliani actually did spend the first night of the New Year with his Greek friends in a bistro in the rue Joseph Bara. Compare also Varvogli's letter, which appears in the Appendix to my essay in Bibl. 85.

# GENERAL BIBLIOGRAPHY

## MONOGRAPHS, MEMOIRS, HOMAGES, AND ARTICLES

1 Bartolini, Luigi. *Modi.* Venice: Edizioni del Cavallino. 1938.

2 Basler, Adolphe. *Modigliani.* Paris: G.Crès. 1931.

3 Carli, Enzo. *Amedeo Modigliani,* preface by Jean Cassou. Rome: De Luca. 1952.

4 Carrieri, Raffaele. *12 Opere di Amedeo Modigliani.* Milan: Edizioni del Milione. 1947.

5 Cartier, Jean-Albert. *Modigliani, nus.* Paris: Fernand Hazan. 1958.

6 Ceroni, Ambrogio. *Amedeo Modigliani, peintre* (with accompanying English text, translated by Van Rensselaer White). Milan: Edizioni del Milione. 1958.

7 ——. *Amedeo Modigliani; dessins et sculptures.* Milan: Edizioni del Milione. 1965.

8 Cocteau, Jean. *Modigliani.* London: A.Zwemmer and Paris: Fernand Hazan. 1950.

9 Dale, Maud. *Modigliani.* New York: Alfred A.Knopf. 1929.

10 Descargues, Pierre. *Amedeo Modigliani.* Paris: Braun et Cie. 1951.

11 Franchi, Raffaello. *Modigliani.* Florence: Arnaud. 1942 (3d ed., 1946).

12 Jedlicka, Gotthard. *Modigliani.* Erlenbach-Zurich: E.Rentsch. 1953.

13 Lipchitz, Jacques. *Amedeo Modigliani.* New York: Harry N.Abrams. 1952.

14 Marchiori, Giuseppe. *Amedeo Modigliani.* Milan: Edizioni del Milione. 1949.

15 Modigliani, Jeanne. *Modigliani: Man and Myth.* New York: The Orion Press. 1958.

16 Nicholson, Benedict. *Modigliani, Paintings.* London: Lindsay Drummond and Paris: Editions du Chêne. 1948.

17 Pavolini, Corrado. *Modigliani.* New York: New American Library. 1966.

18 Pfannstiel, Arthur. *Modigliani,* preface by L.Latourettes. Paris: Marcel Seheur. 1929.

19 ——. *Modigliani et son oeuvre.* Paris: Bibliothèque des Arts. 1956.

20 ——. *Dessins de Modigliani.* Lausanne: Mermod. 1958.

20a Ponente, Nello. *Modigliani.* Florence: Edizioni Sadea. 1969.

21 Raynal, Maurice. *Modigliani.* Geneva: Skira. 1951.

22 Roy, Claude. *Modigliani.* Geneva: Skira. 1958.

23 Russoli, Franco. *Modigliani,* foreword by Jean Cocteau. Milan: Silvana Editoriale d'Arte and New York: Harry N.Abrams. 1958.

24 ——. *Modigliani.* Milan: Fratelli Fabbri. 1963.

25 Salmon, André. *Modigliani, sa vie et son oeuvre.* Paris: Editions des Quatre Chemins. 1926.

26 Salmon, André. *Amedeo Modigliani,* afterword by Jeanne Modigliani. Zurich: Diogenes Verlag. 1960.

27 San Lazzaro, Gualtiero di. *Modigliani, peintures.* Paris: Editions du Chêne. 1947. (Revised ed., 1953.)

28 San Lazzaro, Gualtiero di. *Modigliani, portraits.* Paris: Editions Fernand Hazan. 1957.

29 Schaub-Koch, Emile. *Amedée Modigliani.* Paris and Lille: Mercure Universel. 1933.

30 Scheiwiller, Giovanni. *Amedeo Modigliani.* Milan: U.Hoepli. 1927 (5th ed., 1950).

31 ——. *Modigliani.* Zurich: Der Arche. 1958.

32 Schwarz, Marck. *Amedeo Modigliani.* Paris: Le Triangle. 1927.

33 Sichel, Pierre. *Modigliani.* New York: Dutton. 1967.

34 Taguchi, S. *Modigliani.* Tokyo: Atelier-Sha Éditeur. 1936.

35 Valsecchi, Marco. *Amedeo Modigliani.* Milan: Garzanti. 1955.

36 Vitali, Lamberto. *Disegni di Modigliani.* Milan: U.Hoepli. 1929 (2nd ed., 1936).

37 ——. *Quarantacinque disegni di Modigliani.* Turin: Einaudi. 1959.

38 Werner, Alfred. *Modigliani Sculpteur.* Geneva, Paris, Hamburg: Editions Nagel and New York: Arts, Inc., 1962 *(Modigliani the Sculptor).*

39 ——. *Amedeo Modigliani.* New York: Harry N.Abrams. 1967.

## EXHIBITION CATALOGUES

40 Atlanta. *Modigliani.* 1960.

41 *Modigliani,* introduction by Ch.-A.Cingria. Basel, Kunsthalle. 1934.

42 *Modigliani, Campigli, Sironi,* introduction by A.Rüdlinger. Bern, Kunsthalle. 1955.

43 *Modigliani,* preface by M.Dale. Brussels, Palais des Beaux-Arts. 1933.

44 Brussels. *De Toulouse-Lautrec à Chagall.* 1956.

45 *Modigliani, Drawings from the Collection of Stefa and Leon Brillouin.* Cambridge, Mass., Fogg Art Museum, Harvard University. 1959.

46 *Drawings by Amedeo Modigliani, From the Collection of Mr. and Mrs. J.W.Alsdorf.* Chicago, The Art Institute of Chicago. 1955.

47 *Amedeo Modigliani; Paintings, Sculpture and Drawings,* foreword and catalogue by A.T.Schoener. Cincinnati, The Contemporary Arts Center, Cincinnati Art Museum. 1959.

48 *Amedeo Modigliani,* by E.Rathke and W.George. Frankfurt am Main, Kunstverein. 1963.

49 Hamburg; Kunsthalle. *Die Französische Zeichnung des 20.Jahrhunderts.* 1959.

50 Lausanne; Galerie Vallotton. *Exposition de dessins.* 1961.

51 *Onoranze a Modigliani.* Leghorn, Museo Civico. 1955.

52 *Matisse and Modigliani Drawings.* London, Hanover Gallery. 1962.

53 *Modigliani,* introduction by J.Russell. London, Arts Council of Great Britain. 1963.

54 London; Marlborough-Gerson Gallery. *French Drawings.* 1966.

55 Madrid, Barcelona, San Sebastian, Marseilles. *Mostra d'Arte Italiana Contemporanea.* 1955.

56 *Mostra di Modigliani,* introduction by L.Vitali. Milan, Associazione fra gli Amatori e i cultori delle Arti Figurative Contemporanee. 1946.

57 *Mostra di Amedeo Modigliani,* ed. F.Russoli. Milan: Ente Manifestazioni Milanesi. 1958.

58 Milan; Palazzo Reale. *Arte Italiana del XX Secolo da Collezioni Americane.* 1960.

59 *Modigliani,* by L. Venturi, M. Latour, and J. A. Cartier. Marseilles, Musée Cantini. 1958.

60 *Modigliani; Paintings Drawings Sculpture,* text by J. T. Soby. New York, Museum of Modern Art. 1951 (3d ed., 1963).

61 Paris; Galerie des Quatre Chemins. *Modigliani.* 1926.

62 Paris; Galerie Marcel Bernheim. *Modigliani.* 1931.

63 Paris; Petit Palais. *Collection Girardin.* 1954.

64 *Cent Tableaux de Modigliani,* foreword by R. Nacenta, prefaces by L. Venturi and J. Lassaigne. Paris, Galerie Charpentier. 1958.

65 *Amedeo Modigliani* (Esposizione Nazionale Quadriennale d'Arte 6), introduction and catalogue by E. Carli. Rome: De Luca. 1952.

66 *Modigliani* (La Mostra ... alla Galleria Nazionale d'Arte Moderna), introduction by P. Bucarelli, catalogue by N. Ponente. Rome: Editalia. 1959.

67 Tokyo and Kyoto. *Modigliani,* catalogue by Atsuo Imaizumi, texts by R. Nacenta and K. Nakayama.

68 Washington; Phillips Collection. *Masters of Modern Italian Art from the Collection of Gianni Mattioli.* 1967/68.

OTHER BOOKS AND ARTICLES CITED
IN THE CATALOGUE RAISONNÉ

69 *Anthologie du dessin français au XXᵉ siècle.* Geneva: Cailler. 1951.

70 Arcangeli, Francesco. *Maestro del disegno contemporaneo in una raccolta privata d'arte moderna a Milano.* Milan: All'Insegna del Pesce d'Oro. 1961.

71 Carrieri, Raffaele. *Il disegno italiano contemporaneo.* Milan: Damiani. 1945.

72 Crespelle, J. P. *Montparnasse vivant.* Paris. 1962.

73 d'Ancona, Paolo. *Modigliani Chagall Soutine Pascin: Some Aspects of Expressionism.* Milan: Edizioni del Milione. 1952.

74 Gengaro, Maria Luisa. "A Proposito della datazione di un disegno di Modigliani," in *Scritti di storia dell'arte in onore di Mario Salmi,* vol. 3. Rome: De Luca. 1963.

75 Kueny, Gabrielle and Viatte, Germain. *Grenoble, Musée de Peinture et de Sculpture. Dessins modernes.* Paris: Editions des Musées Nationaux. 1963.

76 Maltese, Corrado. "Per un ripensamento di Modigliani," *Bollettino d'Arte,* Rome, XLIV, series IV, 1. January-March, 1959.

77 Modesti, R. *Pittura Italiana Contemporanea.* Milan: A. Vallardi. 1958.

78 Neugass, Fritz. "Modigliani," in *L'Amour de l'Art,* Paris, 12 May, 1931.

79 Ragghianti, Carlo L. *Arte moderna in una raccolta italiana,* Milan: Edizioni del Milione. 1953.

80 ——. "Modigliani, 1918–1958," *Sele Arte,* Florence, VII, 37. September-October, 1958.

81 ——. "Revisione di Modigliani," *Sele Arte,* Florence, VII, 40. March-April, 1959.

82 Raimondi, Giuseppe. "Amedeo Modigliani," *Comunità,* Milan, XIII, 68. 1959.

83 Rötlisberger, Marcel. "Les Cariatides de Modigliani," *Critica d'Arte,* Florence, VII, 38. 1960.

84 ——. "Modigliani e la critica," in *La Biennale di Venezia,* Venice. 1958.

85 Russoli, Franco. "Per un catalogo dell'opera di Modigliani," in *Scritti di storia dell'arte in onore di Mario Salmi,* vol. 3, Rome. 1963.

86 ——. "Modigliani e il disegno," *Pirelli,* Milan, XX, 4. 1967.

87 Trier, Eduard. *Zeichner des 20. Jahrhunderts.* Berlin: Verlag Gebr. Mann. 1956.

88 Vitali, Lamberto. "Modigliani," in *Preferenze.* Milan: Domus. 1950.

OTHER PUBLICATIONS DEDICATED SPECIFICALLY TO THE
DRAWINGS OF MODIGLIANI

89 *Modigliani: the Sydney G. Biddle Collection,* preface by G. Biddle. New York, Perls Gallery. 1956.

90 Earp, T. W. "London Exhibitions," *Drawing and Design,* London, II, 7. January, 1927.

91 Jedlicka, Gotthard. "Die Zeichnung von Modigliani," *Neue Zürcher Zeitung,* Zurich. January 18, 1934.

92 Venturi, Lionello. "Sulla linea di Modigliani," *Poligono,* Milan. February, 1930.

93 "Un Carnet inédit de Modigliani au Musée d'Art moderne," *Art de France,* Paris. 1964.

# PHOTO CREDITS